AF207534

Millard Fillmore Caldwell

FLORIDA IN FOCUS

UNIVERSITY PRESS OF FLORIDA

Florida A&M University, Tallahassee
Florida Atlantic University, Boca Raton
Florida Gulf Coast University, Ft. Myers
Florida International University, Miami
Florida State University, Tallahassee
New College of Florida, Sarasota
University of Central Florida, Orlando
University of Florida, Gainesville
University of North Florida, Jacksonville
University of South Florida, Tampa
University of West Florida, Pensacola

MILLARD FILLMORE CALDWELL

GOVERNING ON
THE WRONG SIDE
OF HISTORY

GARY R. MORMINO

FOREWORD BY ANDREW K. FRANK

UNIVERSITY PRESS OF FLORIDA

Gainesville / Tallahassee / Tampa / Boca Raton

Pensacola / Orlando / Miami / Jacksonville / Ft. Myers / Sarasota

NOT FOR RESALE
REVIEW COPY ONLY

COPYRIGHT 2020 BY GARY R. MORMINO

All rights reserved

Published in the United States of America

25 24 23 22 21 20   6 5 4 3 2 1

Library of Congress Control Number: 2019954696

ISBN 978-0-8130-6650-9

The University Press of Florida is the scholarly publishing agency for the State
University System of Florida, comprising Florida A&M University, Florida Atlantic
University, Florida Gulf Coast University, Florida International University, Florida State
University, New College of Florida, University of Central Florida, University of Florida,
University of North Florida, University of South Florida, and University of West Florida.

UNIVERSITY PRESS OF FLORIDA

2046 NE Waldo Road

Suite 2100

Gainesville, FL 32609

http://upress.ufl.edu

CONTENTS

FOREWORD

Millard Fillmore Caldwell: Governing on the Wrong Side of History is the second volume in a series devoted to introducing the breadth and diversity of Florida history to the public. Each book presents readers with contemporary interpretations of both new and old topics in the state's history. Lively in prose and shorter than most traditional monographs, the books in Florida in Focus offer anecdotally rich introductions to a series of topics. They tell their stories from original archival sources and place their subjects in local, regional, and hemispheric contexts. Volumes cover the chronological spectrum of Florida's history, and they focus on specific events, places, institutions, people, and themes in its past. The tightly focused books are all written by established scholars, and the works reflect their experience in and outside of the classroom.

The series meets the growing demand for public-facing scholarship. The books are not simply traditional monographs in condensed form. Nor are they summaries of topics that are already known. Instead, each book seeks to create a dialogue with public audiences, presenting them with newly discovered knowledge and introducing them directly to the nature of traditional academic research. Each book asks readers to grapple with the current implications of the past, implicitly and explicitly pointing to ways that the past continues to influence and inform the present.

In *Millard Fillmore Caldwell: Governing on the Wrong Side of History*, Gary Mormino presents the history of one of Florida's most successful politicians, successful at least in terms of winning elections and holding office. Millard Fillmore Caldwell never lost an election, winning a seat as a Democratic state senator in 1929 and a term as a wartime governor in 1944. Upon leaving office, he continued to serve as a public official in a series of positions that included a place on the state's supreme court. His career stretched over a time of great transformation, when Florida went from a mostly rural state committed to segregation to one of the fastest growing states that was increasingly integrated and cosmopolitan.

Despite the changes in Florida and the nation as a whole, Caldwell remained steadfast to his core convictions. His political successes, in many ways, reflected this commitment and, in many ways, reflected the political history of the state in the middle of the twentieth century. Throughout his career, Caldwell was a leading defender of the Jim Crow segregationist South. He defended the lynching of African Americans and the continuation of the white primary. In the face of a strengthening civil rights movement he repeatedly made his opposition and general disrespect for African Americans clear. He also decried what he saw as a cultural decline after World War II. He was, as Mormino explains, resisting the changes that were increasingly transforming Florida and the nation as a whole. In the end, Mormino asks us to consider how we should remember and reconsider a man who spent his career "governing on the wrong side of history."

Andrew K. Frank
Series Editor

INTRODUCTION

Millard Fillmore Caldwell possessed the glamour and confidence of a matinee idol. He rode horses in California, lassoed calves in Texas, and filibustered on the floor of the U.S. Capitol. Hollywood could easily have cast him as Gary Cooper's double in *High Noon,* or Alan Ladd's *Shane,* though not as the role model for Atticus Finch in *To Kill a Mockingbird.* Endowed with a tall frame and blessed with a commanding presence and an economy of speech, he was also wealthy, by dint of inheritance and intelligence. Dashingly handsome with an aristocratic countenance, he lived a comfortable life as a wealthy lawyer and country gentleman who never lost touch with the common folk. Politically, he was a Yellow-Dog Democrat, a Cracker-folk saying meaning that many Floridians would sooner vote for a cur dog than a Republican! Philosophically, he was a Jeffersonian Republican who would have been comfortable on a tobacco farmstead in colonial Virginia. His ancestors fought in the American Revolution. His family owned cotton plantations in Mississippi and ranches in California. A patrician, he wore his conservatism like Roman breastplate.

Caldwell was a Democratic congressman at the birth of the New Deal but resigned due to his dislike of President Franklin D. Roosevelt and his disapproval of big government. Elected governor of Florida during World War II, Caldwell defended lynching, but championed progressive educational reform. He defied conservative lobbyists over the issue of regressive state taxes but defended the constitutionality of the White Primary. While he may have loathed campaigning for office, he was a natural, never losing a single election. No Floridian ever held so many important positions after he left the governor's mansion.

In 1950, Caldwell provided a convenient target for civil rights leaders when, nominated as the first director of the Federal Civil Defense Administration by President Truman, the nominee refused to address black leaders respectfully. As a Florida Supreme Court judge and private citizen in the 1960s and 1970s, Caldwell played the role of a wrathful Moses scolding a sinful society about cultural excesses, judicial overreach, and political liberalism.

Millard Caldwell exuded confidence, seeming to care little what voters or political leaders in his own party or state thought of him. His life could have inspired the role model for America's "tradition-directed man." David Riesman's *The Lonely Crowd* (1950) seemed pitch perfect in a postwar America with its expanding middle classes—"other-directed men"—seeking or accepting conformity. To Americans, exhausted from decades of identity and hyphenated politics, belonging became an end. Raised in a tradition-directed community and time, Caldwell understood his position, place, and sense of responsibility. Core principles— the Bible's parables and country proverbs, family values and heroic role models—guided Millard through life's passages. A Tennessean, he memorized Davy Crockett's adage: "Be sure you're right, then go ahead."

Caldwell idolized another Tennessean, Andrew Jackson, and adopted Old Hickory's cocksure political practices and social graces. "To the victors go the spoils," he reminded disappointed job-seekers. Jackson and Caldwell rarely apologized, reconciled, or backed down from a fight. Core values served as an "internal gyroscope." Other-directed men maneuvered through life equipped with a "radar," more concerned with belonging and being popular. Few political figures seemed less interested in whether voters liked him than Caldwell. Blunt, his handshake measured his manhood and assured his word. He needed neither consultants nor pollsters. Refusing to adjust his hidebound attitudes toward race and the role of the federal government in a rapidly changing state and society left him vulnerable to criticism.[1]

He was the last Florida governor born in the nineteenth century and the first to govern in the atomic age. But while Caldwell's political instincts were unerring, his attitudes toward race and citizenship strike today's Americans as embarrassing, even shocking. He is a classic example of one of the inherent contradictions of leadership. Americans like men and women who remain faithful to their core convictions. But what happens when such convictions turn out to be on the wrong side of history? In Caldwell's case, he remained unapologetic, even dogmatic, about segregation, insisting that the Southern way of life must not change. He was tone deaf on the most significant issue of the twentieth century: racial justice.

The date was 1944, and Melpomene, Thalia, and Clio—the Muses of Tragedy, Comedy, and History—hovered over the Old Vic in London. Laurence Olivier, thirty-seven years old and in his prime, prepared for a dream role aimed to stir British souls in trying times. He would direct and star in *Henry V*, Shakespeare's play about foreign wars, patriotism, and manhood. But first he was committed to play the dashing Major Sergius in George Bernard Shaw's *Arms and the Man*. After watching the play, the Irish theatrical director Tyron Guthrie came backstage. He asked the star, "Don't you *love* Sergius?" Olivier shrugged at the question, "Decidedly not!" Guthrie responded icily, "Well, of course, if you can't love him, you'll never be any good in him, will you?" Three years later, King George VI knighted Olivier, who became the first British actor to receive a life peerage. He later reflected Guthrie had provided him a priceless lesson in acting.[2]

As the biographer of Millard Fillmore Caldwell, I confess to admiring many of the subject's qualities, but abhorring others. I applaud his pride in military service and civic duty, but recoil at his political stubbornness and racial insensitivities. A fascinating subject who lived in turbulent times, he was also a willing prisoner of his time and place. Were Caldwell to read my reservations, he would surely quote Martin Luther, who defiantly proclaimed at the Diet of Worms in 1521, "Here I stand! I can do no other."

1

CHILD OF PRIVILEGE, BOUND TO DUTY

1897–1943

On the seventh of November 1942, the future appeared muddled for Millard Fillmore Caldwell. He had already packed much into his forty-five years. He had enlisted in the Great War and served as Florida state legislator and a U.S. congressman. But his only son had recently died in a tragic accident. He had also resigned his safe congressional seat and moved his family to a Florida farmstead near Tallahassee. Most dramatically, the United States was at war, and victory was not at all assured. Caldwell volunteered, but he was rejected, a combination of age and athletic injuries.

With one eye focused upon front-page headlines of German U-boats mauling Allied ships in the Atlantic, the Battle of Guadalcanal, and the landing of American troops at North Africa, Caldwell turned to the Battle of Valley Forge and the American Revolution. He spent the day filling out an application for the National Society of the Sons of the American Revolution. He took pride in being a descendent of William Sumter, a Virginia patriot. Born in 1731 in Albemarle County, Virginia, he was Millard Caldwell's great-great-grandfather. Captain Sumter, an Englishman, was an indentured servant who sold his services for passage to America. He took part in the great migration west, dying in Burke County, North Carolina, in 1828. His fourteen-year-old son, Thomas Sumter, enlisted as a private in a North Carolina regiment in the American Revolution. He was a fifer—emblematic of Archibald Willard's iconic painting, *Spirit of '76*.[1]

The Caldwell family line is also descended from Hugh Caldwell Jr., born in 1740 in Northern Ireland. He married Ruth Holstein in 1775 in Virginia. Hugh served as a private in the American Revolution and following the war was appointed constable in Botetourt, in the Roanoke region of southwestern Virginia. His son, Hugh Caldwell I, born in 1796 in Bedford, Virginia, married Lucretia Welch in 1925 in Knox County, Tennessee. Their son, Hugh II was born in 1827 in Tennessee and died in 1906 in Knox County. He listed his occupation in the 1850 and 1860 censuses as "farmer." In 1860, the census indicated that Hugh and his wife, Polly Bayless, had moved to Raccoon Valley in Union County, in eastern Tennessee. Hugh and Polly named one of their sons after President Millard Fillmore. The Caldwells typified the Scots-Irish experience, leaving Virginia on the well-trod trail to Tennessee. In his magisterial book, *Albion's Seed*, David Hackett Fischer points out that not all Scots-Irish settlers lived lives of backcountry poor whites. Among the Scots-Irish elites in Virginia, the Carolinas, and Tennessee, the Polks, Jacksons, Calhouns, and Caldwells became prosperous farmers and planters, part of the ruling class.[2]

Born in 1856, Millard Fillmore Caldwell I was named after Millard Fillmore. Why? Millard Fillmore ran as vice president with Zachary Taylor as head of the Whig ticket. He succeeded Taylor when "Old Rough and Ready" died in office in 1850. Fillmore presided over the disintegration of the Whig Party and in 1856 ran for president on the Know Nothing Party ticket. The Know Nothings appealed to Americans alienated by immigrants, especially Irish Catholics. Fillmore was also an adamant Unionist, a quality that appealed to the Caldwell family.[3]

Born 6 February 1897 in Beverly, near Knoxville, Tennessee, Millard Caldwell was the son of a distinguished southern family that had enjoyed success in law, magazine publishing, and farming. Beverly is one of the small communities north of Knoxville in a hilly region of eastern Tennessee. Situated in Grassy Valley, Beverly was settled by small farmers, most of them Scots-Irish. Many of the original settlers described their small landholdings as "plantations." Eastern Tennessee was stubbornly a region apart from the Deep South, known for its large slave plantations. The Caldwells, like other successful families, invested in cotton lands in western Tennessee and northern Mississippi. The Caldwells owned five plantations, ranches, and landholdings ranging from California and New Mexico to Texas, Mississippi, Tennessee, and Florida. His mother, Martha Jane Clapp, was born in Union County, Tennessee, in 1859. His father, Millard Fillmore Caldwell I, was born in Knox County, Tennessee, in 1856. The timing of the name is significant. In 1856, Millard Fillmore ran for the presidency again, this time as a candidate for the American Know Nothing Party. Caldwell's family included a brother, Roscoe, and two sisters, Jeanne Elizabeth and Jamie. For unknown reasons, Millard Fillmore Caldwell never adopted the title Jr. from his father, Millard Fillmore Caldwell I.[4]

As a young boy, Millard traveled extensively, spending a winter on the Mexican border, some time in Virginia, and three years on the family's California ranch in the Sacramento Valley, where he attended a one-room school. He enjoyed a life of privilege—private tutors and a stable of riding horses—but a lasting memory was a teacher at a one-room schoolhouse. "She was as mean as gar broth, but a great teacher." To the manor born, Caldwell took pride in his ability to speak "cracker." A protean term, cracker refers to poor southern whites. In this case, gar is as inedible as it is grotesque—a long, scaly fish with a beak. Since only the poorest Floridians ate gar, a prehistoric-looking fish, "gar broth" would have been an acquired taste.[5]

Millard enrolled at the Baptist-affiliated Carson-Newman College in Jefferson City, Tennessee, where his father had graduated. Six feet, three inches tall, he starred on the 1913–1914 football, basketball, baseball, and track teams. His biography on the Florida Supreme Court website contains what must be the oddest sentence describing a chief justice: "His hotheaded spirit on the field resulted in his dismissal in 1915." He left school apparently after a legendary baseball brawl. Leaving Tennessee following the donnybrook, he enrolled at the University of Mississippi. The 1917–18 *Ole Miss* yearbook depicts Caldwell as a member of the University Law Club and Kappa Sigma fraternity. He also played tackle on the football team and pitched for the Rebels' baseball squad. He reveled in retelling the tale of a pigskin game against then-vaunted Sewanee College on a literal rocky top in Tennessee, where the Purple Tigers thrashed the Rebels, 69–7.[6]

The Great War in Europe fanned patriotic fire across the South, and Millard Caldwell enlisted as a private in the Army in 1918 and was commissioned as a second lieutenant in the 23rd Company Field Artillery. Many of the vital records for WWI veterans were destroyed by fire, and it seems unlikely that Caldwell crossed the ocean considering he was mustered out of military service in January 1919. Caldwell enrolled at the University of Virginia Law School, graduating in 1921.[7]

Arrival in Florida

Millard passed the Tennessee bar exam and briefly practiced law while running a cotton plantation in Macon, Mississippi, before his father asked him to clear title and oversee the family's timberlands in Santa Rosa County, Florida. Bordering Escambia County in the western Panhandle, Santa Rosa County numbered 14,599 inhabitants in 1925, a population largely white and native-born, mostly drawn from Alabama and Georgia. The distance between Milton, the capital seat of Santa Rosa County and Mobile, Alabama, was about sixty miles, with roads largely unpaved across primitive bridges. Driving to Tallahassee required traversing 178 miles of forest. Prior to this era, Santa Rosa's yellow pine forests were far more valuable than the long stretches of pristine gulf beaches. In 1851, a correspondent for the *Baltimore Sun,* described Milton as a bustling town of "three sawmills running 99 saws, and three confectionaries . . ." But Caldwell's arrival coincided with "the passing of the pine," the depletion of the once inexhaustible forests. By 1925, many African Americans had left the impoverished Panhandle as participants in the Great Migration.[8]

Caldwell moved to Milton in 1924. "I never intended to stay in Florida," he later remembered. "I didn't see my future here. I was sorry I came." His father had purchased several thousand acres sight unseen. Falling cotton prices and the agricultural depression threatened the family's far-flung holdings. In Caldwell's words, "Cotton prices were down, taxes were up, and labor was leaving for the North." The Florida land boom of the early 1920s ignited a building frenzy across South Florida, but West Florida languished as agricultural prices fell, a crisis made worse with the collapse of the land boom in 1926.[9]

Millard joined the law firm of Judge and State Senator Sheppard W. Clark. Quickly, he flung himself into the local political arena, serving as city attorney, and later as attorney for the Santa Rosa County Commission. He also befriended neighbors. Historian Brian Rucker relates that his grandfather had a farm a few miles from the Caldwell home, and as a child, he rode on the back of the Caldwell family mule.[10]

When the ambitious young lawyer was not in the courtroom, he was busy courting the love of his life. On Valentine's Day, 1925, Millard Caldwell married Mary Harwood, whom he first met as a young boy in Virginia. The Harwoods lived across the river from the Caldwells, in Saluda, Middlesex County. To squire Mary, Millard had to cross a "pretty sorry" old bridge. He reminisced, "When you trotted your horse across it, it clattered like a honky-tonk on Saturday night." On their wedding day, Mary outranked Millard. She had been appointed superintendent of King George County schools, becoming the first Virginia woman to be elevated to that position. Not until the 1960s did another woman hold such an office in Virginia.[11]

The young couple settled in Milton, a mill town of 2,190 inhabitants on the Blackwater River. There, Mary taught school and acted as a home demonstration agent, introducing canning techniques to poor, rural families.

Caldwell decided to run for state representative in 1928, largely because he disliked the incumbent. "I had my work cleared up in the law office," he reminisced decades later, "and I figured a political campaign was as good a way as any to say the things I wanted to get said." His political career began with a stump speech at Chumuckla Springs. Characteristically, Caldwell offered few promises other than he would be beholden to no one. "After I was finished," he recalled, the publisher of the *Milton Gazette* came up to me and said, "That was the worst political speech I ever heard. You made every man, woman, and child present, including myself, madder than hell." The publisher who had first urged Caldwell to run for office finished his tirade, "There is not a vote left in the audience." Caldwell shrugged, explaining, "I was telling them [audience] what they needed to know. I wasn't consumed by the desire to be elected in the legislature anyway. But I was elected."[12]

Caldwell prided himself as a plainspoken politician. "I never cared much about politics and I guess that showed," he recalled. "His independence was in some ways disturbing," remembered Florida Supreme Court Justice and friend B. K. Roberts. The brash thirty-two-year-old maverick candidate so alienated Governor Doyle Carlton that the chief executive campaigned in Santa Rosa County to defeat the upstart Caldwell. Notwithstanding Carlton's wrath, Caldwell won reelection in 1930 to the State House. Richard W. Ervin served in the 1931 session as the Engrossing Clerk of the Florida House of Representatives. Ervin, future Chief Justice of the Florida Supreme Court, remembered Caldwell:

> He was tall, angular, and rawboned. He had a gift of sarcasm and tough talk. People respected him because he was all no-nonsense, spoke his mind, and believed in being frugal. When he spoke in debate, he articulated clearly and effectively without oratorical flourishes or forensic imagery. He never catered or palavered to anyone. It astounded everyone that he was so popular politically.[13]

Malcolm B. Johnson, the longtime editor of the *Tallahassee Democrat,* wrote about the tumultuous Florida Legislature during the era 1929–1933. "Upstairs in the House of Representatives," he recounted, "was Millard Caldwell and a group of the surest-footed rising young politicians Florida ever had: Claude Pepper, Ed Larson, Fuller Warren, John Mathews, Tom Watson and others destined to go high." Legislators had to confront many crises. "Caldwell was a leader of the Little County bloc and won the fight over state gas tax allocations."[14]

The accomplishments of the Little County bloc wrought enormous political consequences, none greater than the fight over pari-mutuel wagering and the question over how to distribute revenues. In his memoir, Congressman Kenneth "Buddy" McKay recalled, "The compromise that had made gambling acceptable in rural, churchgoing North Florida was that although racetracks could only be situated in counties that had approved them by a subsequent vote, racetrack revenues were to be distributed equally among all counties." In other words, backwoods Baptists and small-town Methodists condemned the sinful ways of the big cities and Gold Coast, while rural legislators could boast of keeping taxes low. "This so-called Eleventh Amendment," remembered McKay, "was said to be somewhere in the Old Testament."[15]

The 1931 Florida legislature—which set a record for lasting one hundred days—confronted issues great and small. Caldwell fondly recalled his vain efforts to kill a proposed barber board. He offered the following amendment: "Each member, in addition to being a practicing barber, shall also be a Doctor of Philosophy, a Doctor of Divinity, and a Doctor of Medicine and Surgery, particularly Surgery." His efforts foiled, he offered one final amendment, adding "habitual conversations" to offenses to which a barber's license could be revoked![16]

Congress

In 1932, Caldwell announced his candidacy for the United States House of Representatives. He had agreed to support fellow state legislator, Jackson County's E. Clay Lewis Jr., in his race for Congress. But when Lewis concluded he could not win the election, Caldwell recoiled, "To hell with that, I will run!" He added, "I did not ask and did not get one dime from anybody." The Congressional Third District encompassed a huge swath of territory ranging from the Escambia River to Jefferson County, east of Tallahassee. Crisscrossing the region's bayous and unpaved roads in his Model A Ford, he drove 14,800 miles and delivered 140 speeches in 30 days.[17]

Elected and reelected by comfortable margins, the conservative Caldwell served four terms in Congress, fulminating against the New Deal while shepherding a flow of federal funds to the Florida Panhandle. In 1938, a prominent North Florida newspaper reminded voters, in capital letters, why the congressman must be reelected: "Millard Caldwell is a member of the all-important and powerful Appropriations Committee of the House of Representatives, from which ALL APPROPRIATIONS MUST ORIGINATE, as provided by the Constitution." The paper did not need to explain, "Huge sums of money have been secured for Leon County by Millard Caldwell. . . . More Federal money has been spent in this district since Millard Caldwell became our Congressman than in all the previous history of Florida." His efforts helped create today's Blackwater River State Forest. He used his influence to assist the transfer of lands from the Choctawhatchee National Forest to Eglin Army Air Force Base. "The hand that signs the war contract," a popular saying reminded voters, "is the hand that shapes the future." Congressman Caldwell, curious to understand "what made Mr. Hitler tick," paid his own passage to Europe to visit pre-war Germany.[18]

In photographs of Mary, Millard, and their three children, the young congressman projected a striking image of an all-American family man. He played in the 1933 Congressional World Series, pitching for the Democrats. President Roosevelt threw out the first pitch. But in matters of race and morality, Caldwell was intolerant of alternative lifestyles or challenges to the status quo. In 1936, he wrote the Librarian of the Library of Congress, addressing concerns that the hallowed institution was collecting pornography. Librarian Herbert Putnam replied, admitting that the "Delta Colletcion" [sic] contained such materials, but such items were restricted to adults and could only be read in the Rare Book Room. In May 1937, Congressman Caldwell joined the Florida delegation, voting against the Federal Anti-Lynching bill. U.S. Senator, Claude Pepper, also voted against the bill.[19]

Caldwell maintained relationships with colleagues and staff that lasted for decades. The first-term congressman hired Jacob C. Belin as a young aide. Belin's father was an executive at the St. Joe Paper Company in Port St. Joe. The precocious student at George Washington University befriended Ed Ball and Millard Caldwell. "I have always admired Millard Caldwell," reflected Belin in a 1992 interview. "He was a Tennessean, and there was always something about Caldwell that reminded me a great deal of [Andrew] Jackson and of Lincoln. . . . He was tough. He had his way."

Like Jackson, Caldwell was loyal to his friends. "If you did not vote for him," remembered Belin, "you did not get anything."[20]

In the 1930s, congressional staffs were lean. "There were two and a half full-time employees, the secretary and I guess his administrative assistant and me," recollected Belin. "Caldwell . . . could get on the phone and turn mountains." The young aide also recounted the importance of Caldwell's social network. "Mr. Caldwell would say, all right, so-and-so has a daughter here, and you have a tuxedo. We are going out for dinner."[21]

In 1940, the four-term congressman from Milton announced he would not seek reelection. He confessed in 1981, "I was never very happy with being a Democrat and being opposed to what the party was trying to do." The vacancy opened the door for Robert Sikes, the Crestview "He-Coon" who vaulted from his seat in the Florida legislature to an extraordinary—if not controversial—career in the U.S. House of Representatives (1941–1979). Why would Caldwell leave Congress precisely at such a critical juncture—when Europe and Asia were aflame, and a resurgent federal government was flooding northwest Florida with its largesse? After all, he already sat on the most-coveted committees, at a time when powerful southerners (William B. Bankhead, J. Lister Hill, Sam Rayburn, Wright Patman, John Rankin, Carl Vinson, and Mendel Rivers) ruled Congress.[22]

Leaving Capitol Hill involved personal and political factors. Twelve-year-old Millard Fillmore Caldwell III served as a Congressional page. On 3 February 1939, young Millard was walking to Page School when an automobile struck and killed him, dragging his body fifty feet. Despite a massive manhunt, the driver was never caught. Administrators and classmates dedicated a plaque to young Millard's memory.[23]

The Caldwells never enjoyed Washington, DC. Mary Caldwell was especially happy to leave. Confessing homesickness to a reporter, she explained, "I suppose I never will be anything but a country girl." As a congressman, Caldwell was absent from roll call votes 14.2 percent of his time in Washington, a rate double that of his peers.[24]

Politically, Caldwell was a genuine conservative who opposed the growing encroachment of New Deal policies. Caldwell's feeling about FDR were scathing and frank: "I did not support him [Roosevelt] for the nomination, and I have to this day not discussed Roosevelt's name on the stump . . . I did not like him, and I did not like anything about him." Such candor shocked and disappointed peers. "I left Congress because I was tired of it," he explained years later, adding, "I never liked what Congress was doing. . . . Congress was full of deadbeats." He also disapproved some of the New Deal's most popular programs, such as the Works Progress Administration (WPA). The congressman joined fellow Southerners in opposing the federal anti-lynching legislation. John Wiggington, a law partner, judge, and friend, contended that Caldwell was an "anachronism who was dragged kicking and screaming into the twentieth century. . . . He was born 100 years too late." An Associated Press (AP) biographical sketch of Congressman Caldwell, dated 1934, is revealing. The document explained that it was "intended for use primarily in the event of his death." AP reporters described Caldwell:

> Keen wit and sharp sarcasm—when he wanted to be sarcastic if intended—were characteristics of Millard F. Caldwell. When it came to a battle of wits and words, the tall, broad-shouldered Caldwell neither asked quarter nor gave it.[25]

Caldwell loathed and feared the threat of German fascism and Japanese imperialism. Accordingly, he voted for military appropriations and preparedness, actions that also fortified the Panhandle. The young congressman could also be a visionary. In 1934, he persuaded fellow members to investigate the supply of tin, in case of national emergency. Japan was aggressively hoarding tin supplies. But Caldwell hated Washington politics, its lobbyists, its feeding trough, and the social impact of the New Deal. The *Milton Gazette*, in a none-too-subtle 1942 editorial, asked, "Marianna gets a five-million-dollar air corps training school. . . . Why is Milton almost completely ringed with defense projects and we get nothing?" Ultimately, Milton was rewarded for its patience after Caldwell departed Congress. Naval Auxiliary Air Station Whiting Field was commissioned in July 1943.[26]

Tallahassee

The Caldwells moved to Tallahassee in the early 1940s. "I like Tallahassee," exclaimed Caldwell. "It is the most beautiful town that I know in the entire country. I like the people." Tallahassee in 1940 retained vestiges of the Old South, with its antebellum homes and social manners. Leon County's population had not yet reached 32,000, of whom over half were African American. Written in the late 1930s, *A Guide to the Southernmost State* described Tallahassee: "Red-clay streets intersect many paved thoroughfares, and horse-and mule-drawn vehicles are not uncommon sights." Until the late 1930s, genteel Tallahassee continued to follow the Southern tradition of mourning. A journalist described the proper etiquette of funeral notices. "Dressed in his Sunday best, a negro employed in the family of the deceased would take the notice to the homes of friends and acquaintances." The notice, explained a reporter:

> was a card of fine texture about the size of a magazine cover. A heavy black ribbon was drawn through slits at the top and bottom. It was carried on a silver tray. The servant, dressed in a Prince Albert coat, knocked on doors, presenting the tray to the ladies or gentlemen of the house. Southern manners dictated that friends should not read about neighbors' deaths in a cold, newspaper obituary.[27]

In 1941, Caldwell purchased the Blackwood plantation, located five miles northwest of the city on Bainbridge Road. Colonel Robert Butler built a plantation house on the property in 1826. Butler was Florida's first Surveyor General and a friend of Andrew Jackson. Charles Black acquired the 800-acre-estate in 1828 and died shortly thereafter. His tombstone, located in a rural family cemetery not far from the plantation home reads, "Here, Repose the remains of Charles Black . . . He was a native of Beaufort District South Carolina And came to Florida in the pursuit of Happiness And Wealth." The Black family lived on the property until a yellow fever epidemic scoured the area in 1841. Black's widow, Janet Reid Black, was the daughter of Florida Governor Robert

Raymond Reid. The governor lived on the Blackwood plantation briefly and is buried in the nearby Blackwood-Harwood Plantations Cemetery. The Johnson family sold the property in 1907 to the Florida-Carolina Company, for the purpose of planting a pecan orchard. Originally constructed in 1850 by Rev. George C. Johnson, the two-and-a-half-story house, constructed by slaves with hand-hewn timbers, with original two-inch thick pine floors, served as a comfortable home. The Maryland-born Reverend Johnson was master of a 320-acre plantation. His slaves picked 150 bales of cotton in 1850.[28]

Certain his career in public service was over, the planter's son purchased an 800-acre working plantation. For Caldwell, it was love at first sight. He explained to a reporter in 1968, "In 1924, my father and I were driving across the state from the East Coast to Pensacola. At that time the Old Bainbridge Road was part of the old East-West highway—practically no paving—and we got out there on the Old Bainbridge Road and saw what we thought was an attractive, dilapidated old place and just got out and walked around and thoroughly enjoyed it. I came back in 1940 and bought that place." He purchased the home without inspecting the interior. The new residents included daughters Sally and Susan, along with their adored cats, Petunia and Beelzebub. The new proprietor was not a gentleman farmer, but a serious agriculturist who built up the farm stock to include one hundred dairy cows, forty laying hens, and a flock of turkeys, Tennessee walking horses, as well as a Poland China brood sow and boar. To honor his beloved wife, he named the place Harwood. "As Uncle Eaton used to say," Millard quipped, "I would rather throw rocks at hogs for a living in the country, than to grow rich in the city." But Millard quickly became a well-known figure in downtown Tallahassee. He was a member of the Elks, Freemasons, the Knights of Pythias, and Shriners.[29]

Diane Roberts, a professor of English at Florida State University, grew up as a neighbor of the First Family of Florida. She recalls playing on the Harwood plantation grounds, which included a steephead spring, a slave graveyard, and a possible Spanish mission.[30]

Mary Harwood Caldwell and Millard Caldwell outside their plantation in Leon County. Courtesy State Archives of Florida, Florida Memory. https://www.floridamemory.com/items/show/136832.

A journalist writing in a period style described the matron of Harwood: "Mrs. Caldwell, Harwood's charming hostess, is an attractive brunette of slender build. She has a gracious drawing-room manner and yet at the same time gives the impression that she could probably take over the farm and capably run it in an emergency." Margo Tupper of the *St. Petersburg Times* depicted Mary Caldwell as "tall and athletic yet poised and dainty. She is typically southern and in perfect accord with her surroundings." The reporter added, "The versatile Mrs. Caldwell finds time to make most of her own clothes and those for her two daughters. . . . Her pantry is full of home-grown foods, for she cans everything from figs to turnip greens." Mrs. Caldwell would soon by joined in canning rooms by many American women, as brown figs and collard greens validated the jingle, "Food will win the war!"[31]

War!

For a state that trafficked in dreams, Florida had good reasons to welcome the first Sunday in December 1941. Symbolically and socially, the date marked the unofficial beginning of Florida's tourist season. By Sunday afternoon, 7 December, news of Pearl Harbor shattered the chamber of commerce's visions of Florida beaches filled with tourists. Ironically, out of the maelstrom of war came a huge new stream of visitors, wearing khaki, olive drab, and navy blue.[32]

Pearl Harbor changed everything. Instantly, America and Americans abandoned isolationism and America First, as all efforts were concentrated upon war and victory. Caldwell, a veteran of the Great War, volunteered, but at age forty-five, officials deemed him more valuable on the home front.[33]

"Japan has done one thing for us," proclaimed the *Tallahassee Democrat*. "The cowardly attack . . . has united the nation as nothing else could have done." Seven months later, the same paper noted the transformation of small-town Tallahassee: "War redirects and changes. We are in the midst of war." A surge of patriotism swept the state. To Caldwell, an upper-class gentleman steeped in traditions of Southern honor, a "sneak attack" defined our new enemy.[34]

Florida furnished America with the war's first heroes: Colin P. Kelly and Alexander "Sandy" Nininger. In 1941, Fuller Warren was a young man on the make, an ambitious politician writing a flurry of letters to the editor. "I want to take an active part in slaughtering the Japs and Germans," one letter began. He added, "I have no inclination to kill Italians—whom I consider craven cowards." A Pensacola civic club pledged fifty dollars to the first aviator to drop a bomb on Tokyo; in Gadsden County, civilians contributed to a prize awarded the first local boy to kill a Japanese soldier. News of Lt. Col. Jimmy Doolittle's raid over Tokyo in April 1942 thrilled Floridians, even more so when it was revealed that his crew had trained at Eglin Airfield in Okaloosa County. Caldwell's successor, Congressman Bob Sikes, earned his reputation as a "He-Coon," securing military appropriations for West Florida. The federal government that Caldwell so distrusted disbursed more than $100 million in the Pensacola area in just three years.[35]

The explosive growth of military establishments across Florida underscored the most tangible evidence of war. From a handful of military establishments in 1940, Florida added an extraordinarily diverse collection of facilities ranging from the 165,000 acres of jungle terrain surrounding Camp Gordon Johnston in Carrabelle to the Naval Amphibious Training Base in Fort Pierce, where future frogmen learned to become underwater demolition experts. The Sunshine State became the Garrison State.[36]

Wings over Florida became a familiar sight. In 1939, Florida claimed six aviation schools; by the end of the war, the state boasted forty aviation installations. Lured by year-round flight conditions, cheap land, flat terrain, and aggressive congressmen, the military established or expanded mega air bases from Pensacola to Miami.[37]

The home front war eroded the thin veneer of social cohesion. Shortages, rationing, and a scarcity of housing exacerbated relationships. As late as 1944, the City of Tallahassee celebrated an annual "community picnic." The local paper announced in May 1944, "All families are invited. Each family will bring its own picnic basket . . . If anybody feels the urge to dance while the school orchestra plays, the tennis court may be used for dancing." Social conventions being what they were, the *Daily Democrat* did not need to remind readers that the "community picnic" was for whites only.[38]

2

THE CANDIDATE AND THE GOVERNOR

1943–1949

Not even a world war could derail Florida politics. Through social up-heaval, economic collapse, and world war, America has maintained a tradition of elections. A steady hand and captain, Governor Spessard Holland guided Florida through the first four years of war. When asked in 1981 what governor he most respected, Caldwell thought Spessard Holland had performed admirably in difficult times. The two men might have been twins. Small-town boys, ruggedly handsome and talented athletes, veterans of the Great War, successful lawyers and Tallahassee legislators, Holland and Caldwell were, in the words of Edward Ball, "dyed-in-the-wool conservative Democrats."[1]

What compelled Caldwell's return to the political stage? After all, he enjoyed his comfortable status as a country gentleman, farmer, and small-town lawyer. The answer may have been as simple as old friends encouraging him to enter the gubernatorial race. Caldwell contemplated the contest with the self-assurance and confidence that he had never lost a political contest. Finally, he simply believed in the old-fashioned creed that public service was honorable. Caldwell's father had instilled in his sons the importance of *noblesse oblige,* the obligation of the better social classes to govern. The doctrine also inferred that the privileged classes show generosity and nobility toward the poor and misfortunate. Millard Fillmore Caldwell demonstrated in word and deed his obligation to serve in war and peace.

However, like many Southern leaders, Caldwell lacked sympathy and empathy for the working classes and African Americans. If Caldwell were able to defend himself, he surely would protest, wagging a finger and itching for a fist fight. The Caldwells, he would insist, had earned a reputation in Tennessee as generous masters of the plantation, a condition and quality twenty-first century critics cannot possibly understand or appreciate.

The 1944 gubernatorial race attracted a talented, crowded field. Two well-known politicians announced their candidacies. Ernest R. Graham was a prominent Dade County dairy farmer and state senator, while Congressman Lex Green was a Bradford County native. Caldwell maintained a lifelong Jeffersonian distaste of big cities, and Miami embodied everything Caldwell's North Florida neighbors disliked. Lex Green was a career politician, a practice Caldwell despised, but he admitted, "Lex Green was the man to beat. . . . He was a good campaigner, an excellent campaigner."[2]

Caldwell announced his candidacy in late September 1943. It was an era devoid of long and expensive campaigns, but as the *Tallahassee Daily Democrat* explained, "For years the Democratic nomination in Florida has been tantamount to election." But one first had to win the critical primary and runoff. An underdog, Caldwell faced several formidable opponents in the primaries.[3]

Ernest R. "Cap" Graham represented the growing economic and political power of South Florida. Like most of his Dade County neighbors, Graham came from somewhere else. Born in Michigan in 1885, he earned an engineering degree and operated a gold mine in Deadwood, South Dakota, and served with the 309th Engineers in France during the Great War. He moved to Dade County to grow sugar for the Pennsylvania Sugar Company. The vast sugar plantation abutted a canal that flowed southeast into the Miami River. The great Hurricane of 1926 and the Florida land bust soured corporate plans. When the company ceased operations in Florida, Graham acquired seven thousand acres of land as severance pay which he turned into the Graham Dairy operations. Graham served in the Florida State Senate from 1936 to 1944. A son, Philip, was a University of Florida roommate and fraternity brother to future U.S. Senator George

A. Smathers. A Harvard Law School graduate, Philip clerked in the U.S. Supreme Court. In the momentous year, 1940, Philip married Katherine Meyer, the daughter of Ernest Meyer, owner of the *Washington Post*. He then enlisted in the Army Air Corps. His younger half-brother, Bob, became a future Florida governor and U.S. senator.[4]

Robert Alexis "Lex" Green was born in Union County, located in North Florida. While attending the University of Florida, he served as a messenger and clerk in the Florida House of Representatives. Following graduation, Green taught school and worked as a high school principal in Live Oak. Elected to the Florida House of Representatives in 1918, he opened a law office in Starke in 1921. He served as judge in Bradford County until elected to Congress in 1924. His North Florida constituents reelected Green nine consecutive terms. When announcing his candidacy for governor in late 1943, he was the dean of the Florida congressional delegation, recognized around Washington for his lavish bow ties.[5]

Caldwell burnished an image of an articulate, no-nonsense politician. Newspaper editors, rednecked farmers, and the business classes admired his refreshing frankness. Early in the campaign, he reminded journalists and audiences, "I will not swap promises for votes." He once told a gathering of Jewish voters, "I'm sure you want to hear from me what I will do for Jews. The answer is nothing. I'm not interested in you as Jews, but as citizens." On another occasion, he addressed a gathering of teachers after Lex Green, a former public-school teacher, had promised raises. Caldwell's talk contained few platitudes; rather, he bemoaned the state of public education in general, and teaching. On still another occasion, he appeared at a rally in Graceville attended by several thousand farmers and small-town folk. "Let me tell you every farmer here is going to get a check from Uncle Sam. The big farmers are going to get big checks, and the little farmers are going to get little checks . . . Then let me tell you something. I voted against your getting that check. You have not done a thing to justify it. . . . It is pure politics."[6]

The 1944 Florida gubernatorial campaign combined elements of small-town Main Street. Since Sidney J. Catts had driven his Model T in the

1916 campaign, candidates had crisscrossed the Sunshine State in Fords, Studebakers, and Buicks. Voters and candidates still valued face-to-face meetings. Handbills announced, "Millard F. Caldwell, Candidate for Governor, Will Speak Today to the People of Cedar Key in front of Trawick's Drug Store." In Cocoa, Caldwell spoke at Central Park. His 8 May 1944 expense account listed $3.82 for gas and oil, $1.73 for dinner (which included drinks and a 40-cent tip), and a dime for newspapers.[7]

Rivals Lex Green and Ernest Graham held one important advantage over Caldwell: The former reminded voters he was a proud graduate of the University of Florida, while the latter boasted that his son, an army major, was an alumnus of the flagship university and a member of the prestigious Blue Key society. The Caldwell campaign appealed to Gator alumni in an unusual letter:

Dear Fellow Florida Alumnus:

How would you like a winning football team at the old school for a change? Me, too! It isn't funny the way Georgia, Georgia Tech and the rest have been wiping their cleats on us. What are we, another Sewanee in the Southeastern Conference? The solution, you ask? The chief executive of the state can be of immeasurable assistance in this? If 'the man in Tallahassee' wants a winning football team at Florida he can come as near getting it as any individual. . . . To hell with Georgia—Vote for Caldwell.[8]

No one understood the changing nature of Florida politics better than Allen Morris. A journalist and confidante to politicians, Morris wrote a state-syndicated column between 1940 and 1966 called "Cracker Politics." His April 1944 syndicated column announced, "Running for office in Florida now combines merchandizing methods of chain store and neighborhood grocery." Caldwell, the country patrician who felt comfortable behind a microphone as well as atop a stump, appreciated the power of the media. He was a natural, who adjusted to the changing media. His campaign hired a "skilled professional editor" to produce 16 mm film strips "with Millard Caldwell telling the people of his background and platform, his voice to continue as the scene shifts to lumber mills, shipyards, groves, farms, forests, Bok tower, Silver Springs, Marineland, shipping, etc." An unidentified aide noted, "This is new. It will have the impact like the first sound wagon." Radio scripts detail how Caldwell and his staff targeted specific audiences: veterans, working men, and housewives. "Ladies! Ladies," began one radio advertisement, "Have you voted yet for Millard Caldwell for governor?" Another radio script introduces listeners to a deadbeat who borrows money with broken promises of repayment. The narrator reassures the listener: "This fellow Millard Caldwell we hear is running for Governor . . . They say he never did make a political promise, and we never have been able to find anybody that says he did." North Floridians listened as Caldwell warned them that if elected, Ernest Graham promised he would build a state university in "south Florida"—a blatant threat to the state's existing public universities—none of which were located south of Gainesville. Staffers even considered hiring an astrologist predicting Caldwell's triumph.[9]

Caldwell, or for that matter any elected official, saw no need to reach out to African American voters, since Florida's white primary eliminated black voters in the only election that mattered in a one-party state. In the 1930s, African Americans began shifting party allegiance away from the Republican Party, "the party of Lincoln," to the Democratic Party, "the party of FDR."[10]

But in April 1944, the U.S. Supreme Court declared white primaries unconstitutional. Southerners in general and Floridians running for governor quickly denounced *Smith v. Allwright*, vowing defiance of the judicial decision. Candidate Caldwell declared, "This new menace to the independence of the state and party must be resisted with well-directed energy." A few months later, he explained, "I look at the primary as being similar to a club." Florida's liberal-leaning U.S. Senator Claude Pepper, facing reelection, vowed that the South must "maintain white supremacy."[11]

In May 1944, Floridians went to the polls to vote in the first primary. Political pundits predicted that the runoff would almost certainly be between Graham and either Green or Caldwell. The latter two were expected to split the North Florida vote. The *Tampa Morning Tribune,* among other newspapers, printed headlines the morning after the election that Caldwell was running third in a close race. However, when the ballots were counted, Caldwell received the most votes, followed by Green and Graham. The runoff pitted two North Florida candidates.[12]

Only three weeks separated the two primaries. Caldwell vowed, "I will make no promises, I will engage in no mud-slinging or character attacks against my opponent." He quickly broke his pledge. A popular handbill titled "The Deadly Parallel" mocked his opponent. The flier pointed out that during World War I, Caldwell "enlisted out of college as a private . . . [and served as a] former commander of the American Legion Post of Milton," whereas Green "claimed deferment because he was a clerk in the Florida Legislature, which meets for 60 days every two years." Comparing their Congressional careers, Caldwell "served 8 years (voluntarily retired in 1940)," while Green "served 19 years (received about $200,000 in salary) and was placed on more unimportant committees than any other member of Congress." Still another campaign advertisement depicted Lex Green dressed like Lord Fauntleroy. The ad reads, "The picture tells the story . . . a story of affectation . . . the flowering Windsor tie . . . the sideburns . . . the regalia of a carnival barker, the ballyhoo artist, the showman, the medicine man."[13]

In an era when newspaper endorsements still mattered, Caldwell welcomed favorable editorials. The *St. Petersburg Times,* the state's most liberal newspaper, editorialized, "Candidate Green has become a badly rattled, obviously frightened man. . . . Candidate Caldwell is the same calm, poised, non-promising fellow he was at the beginning of the race. . . . Caldwell is deliberate, calm, studious, responsible—but not reactionary." The *Miami Herald* surprisingly endorsed Caldwell, "In former Congressman Caldwell," the paper wrote, "the people of Florida have a candidate who is qualified by experience, ability, intelligence, vision and practical sound sense to administer the state through the trying period ahead."[14]

Florida voters went to the polls on 23 May and chose Millard Caldwell as the Democratic candidate for governor. He defeated Green by almost forty thousand votes. In the custom of the time, newspapers referred to Caldwell as "governor-elect." The winning candidate had confounded critics, noted the *Tampa Morning Tribune,* running for governor "with a warning that, with an almost completely West Florida background, he probably would prove unacceptable to the big counties and lower east and west counties." Crushed, Green resigned his congressional seat to become a lieutenant commander in the navy.[15]

Caldwell scarcely campaigned in the months between the May primary and November election, rarely mentioning his Republican opponent. A radio address from 11 October 1944 revealed a candidate with one foot in World War II and the other grounded in the War Between the States.

> It is unnecessary to remind you that the United States, of all the nations of the world engaged in this war, is the only one in which a nationwide election is being held. Our dissatisfied friends say the South will prosper more under the Republican Party. We remember, and we may remind them, of the Reconstruction Days when the Republican Party put the Carpet-bagger yoke on our neck—when we were starved, industrially and economically . . .[16]

Election of 1944: Divining the Entrails

On 7 November 1944 Floridians went to the polls. Judged by newspaper coverage and editorials, Floridians' most important issue seemed to be whether to reelect Franklin D. Roosevelt to an unprecedented fourth term. The race for governor, featuring Caldwell against his Republican opponent Bert Leigh Acker, was not even a page-one story. Acker deserved more respect. Boasting a colorful resume, the sixty-two-year-old Republican was born in New York City, had acted in several silent films, and had twice run unsuccessfully for Congress after moving to Miami Beach. His son, First Lt. Bert Acker Jr. received a Silver Star for heroism in Germany.[17]

Florida's Grand Old Party (GOP), still haunted by the ghosts of Reconstruction, struggled mightily to be relevant. The future looked bright, briefly, in 1928, when Republican Herbert Hoover carried Florida by a comfortable margin, as well as winning Texas, North Carolina, South

Carolina, Tennessee, and Virginia. But 1928 was an illusion, an election determined by the Democratic nominee Al Smith's faith (Catholicism). President Roosevelt's New Deal coalition was wildly successful at the national and state levels. The fortunes and future of Florida's Republican Party sank so low that it faced elimination from the official ballot. But in 1937, Democratic legislators passed a bill resetting the minimum number of voters required in the previous election at 15 percent. Why would Democrats throw a lifeline to a sinking party? State Senator Fred L. Touchton of Dade City (Pasco County) explained in graphic terms: "We've got Republicans in Florida, and we can't shoot 'em. We want to keep them out of the Democratic party where they might have the balance of power."[18]

Florida's official party registration numbers for 1942 were so sobering that Republican hopefuls must have thought a decimal point had been moved: 604,341 Floridians had registered as Democrats, while 36,530 residents identified themselves as Republicans. In Baker, DeSoto, Franklin, Indian River, Jefferson, Lafayette, Liberty, and Washington counties, *not a single* Republican had registered or bothered to participate in a fruitless franchise. In Calhoun, Gilchrist, Glades, Hendry, Hernando, Levy, Madison, Okaloosa, Santa Rosa, St. Lucie, Sumter, Taylor, and Union counties, fewer than one hundred Republicans braved the democratic process. Democrats felt little need to vote in November.[19]

When examining the burnt entrails of 1944, Republicans found a few. Caldwell had received only 61 percent of the vote. Moreover, since the 1920s, the GOP's hopes first shone in Pinellas County, as Midwestern transplants brought their isolationist outlook and Republican Party identities with them. In 1944, Republicans constituted about one quarter of the county's registered voters. "The nearest approach to the 'two-party system' in Florida is in Pinellas County," editorialized the *Tampa Morning Tribune* in November 1944. An agitated Pinellas County Democrat, Archie Clement, warned voters, "If you want to commit political suicide so far as getting any state benefits is concerned, you have merely to let just one Republican into the courthouse and get yourself known at Tallahassee as a Republican County."[20]

Governor-elect Caldwell understood that the Solid South and Democratic Party's hegemony in Florida was barely solid and hardly united. Fissures between the slow-growing, rural North and fast-paced, urbanizing South Florida were becoming more pronounced. But new forces challenged the status quo. Most significantly, a war was shaking the South.

Thousands of African American soldiers, many of them raised in the North, challenged Jim Crow law and tradition. Several disturbing racial incidents occurred. A black army colonel wrote Governor Caldwell with a stark view of the Sunshine State: "I had no idea that I would hear of similar acts of Fascism upon return to the great arsenal of democracy, America." Over 227,000 Floridians served in the armed forces, and as many as two million Americans (but also Britons, Russians, and Chinese) arrived in Florida to serve at one of the state's nearly two hundred military bases.[21]

War's hurly-burly recharged Florida, as the state was flooded with federal dollars, construction crews, GI Joes and Janes, displaced dowagers, black-market gamblers, and trailing wives desperate for a last embrace. Florida's urban and rural infrastructure barely coped.

The new governor and citizens expressed both anxiety and gratitude over the increasing waves of federal dollars keeping Florida solvent. The very question of federal aid to Florida had aroused a great debate in the 1930s, splitting the Democratic Party. When the Great Depression ravaged Florida and the nation, Governor Doyle Carlton and the legislature cut spending and reduced services, preaching a philosophy of self-sufficiency and governmental efficiency. Floridians elected David Sholtz governor in 1932, embracing his faith in the New Deal and federal relief. Yet in 1936, Floridians elected Fred Cone, one of the most conservative governors in state history. Washington, regardless of the occupants of Tallahassee's Grove, continued to pump more and more dollars into state and local coffers. The sheer amount of federal aid exploded, rising from $1 million in 1930 to $3.2 million in 1935 to $12.2 million in 1940 to $17.7 in 1945. "After 1935," observed historian William W. Rogers, "Florida evolved past its traditional status as a small-government state. The forces of change were inexorable, and the result was inevitable: complex, complicated government on a scale unable to meet the needs of a grow-ing state." The governor-elect pondered these issues and changes as he prepared to take office in 1945.[22]

Caldwell immersed himself in state government in the months prior to inauguration. "Many Tallahasseeans will tell you," wrote journalist Howard W. Hartley, "Millard Caldwell will set up shop better equipped to handle Florida's toughest job than any predecessor in the state's history." He added, "Certainly few other governors have gone to greater lengths than Caldwell to add up the score on the things the state government must do in riding out the gales of industrial conversion after the guns cease firing."[23]

Governor-elect Caldwell balanced the political spoils tradition of An-drew Jackson with the modern goal of recruiting talented state work-ers. He believed in balancing the old patronage ways with a merit-based system. He rewarded trusted friends and quickly established a reputa-tion for his icy independence and snap judgment. Longtime law partner and political confidante John Wiggington confided that Caldwell was al-ways very loyal to friends. Wiggington recalled a visit by Bernie Papy, a powerful Key West legislator who had opposed Caldwell in 1944. When Papy asked for a favor, Caldwell replied bluntly, "Bernie, when you didn't support me, you shot snake eyes." He summarized: "And that ended the conversation."[24]

Inauguration Day: January 1945

As inaugural day 1945 beckoned, Florida's capital resembled a hive of uni-formed soldiers and college students, city residents and job seekers. Tal-lahassee was bedecked with patriotic bunting. Not since October 1861, when star-crossed John Milton was sworn in as governor had the symbol and presence of war been so omnipresent in Tallahassee and environs. Milton, the son of Homer Virgil Milton, overwhelmed by the burdens of war and the expectation of defeat, committed suicide in April 1865. "Death," he scribbled, was "preferable to reunion."

Had Governor Milton returned to the capital and surrounding environs in 1945, he would have felt at home, pleased to note the martial stirrings and the monuments to the Lost Cause. Today, we may discuss whether Florida is truly a "southern state," and if so, where the invisible line of demarcation between the North and South dissects the Sunshine State; but in 1945 old times here had not been forgotten in America's southernmost State. Across Florida, marble and granite obelisks and statues of Johnny Reb lined courthouse squares; fourteen Confederate veterans and 536 widows of Confederate soldiers still received $40 monthly pensions; and each 26 April, school children attending Robert E. Lee, Nathan Bedford Forrest, Edmund Kirby Smith, T. J. Jackson, and John Jackson Dickison schools, among others, read verses dedicated to the fallen warriors. In Washington, DC, visiting Floridians paused to pay respect to native son General Edmund Kirby Smith in the Capitol's Statuary Hall.[25]

In Tallahassee, two Civil War cannons guarded the entrance to the Capitol. On 2 January 1945, as inaugural crowds began to gather, a legislator nervously noted that the cannons faced the people, the democracy. The solon promised to introduce a bill requiring the cannons to face down the government.[26]

In January 1945, the war's weary toll weighed heavily upon Floridians. One reporter observed that the inauguration's gaiety "was subdued by the somber tread of marching soldiers from Camp Gordon Johnston." Customarily, the new governor nominated friends and donors as honorary colonels, but Caldwell declined the practice because of the weary war mood. Capital-city residents understood the observation of a *Tallahassee Democrat* reporter: "On every street, in each store, and in the homes, there is some reminder of the war." Fewer cars crowded city streets, in part, because of gas rationing, in part, because the sheriff had asked local citizens "to leave their autos at home."[27]

As longtime residents gathered to hear Florida's twenty-ninth governor, they observed many new faces that had arrived to work in the capital. They also noticed the absence of old faces. One-third of the city's lawyers and one-half of the city's police force had enlisted in the service, as had state legislators. The site of the greatest concentration of single women

The First Family of Florida, Inaugural Day, January 3, 1945. Courtesy State Archives of Florida, Florida Memory. https://www.floridamemory.com/items/show/16489.

south of Washington, DC, Florida State College for Women enrollment spiked during the war years, whereas enrollment at the male-only University of Florida had plunged. Weekends brought hitchhiking soldiers from Tallahassee's Dale Mabry Airfield and Carrabelle's Camp Gordon Johnston, desperate for female companionship.[28]

Tallahassee's vibrant black neighborhood, Frenchtown, as well as Florida A&M College, served as magnets for the region's African American troops. In August 1944, two hundred black soldiers protested the arrest of five black servicemen in Frenchtown on charges of disorderly conduct. African American troops surrounded the MPs, demanding that the accused men surrender to "colored military police."[29]

But on 3 January 1945, Tallahassee became a center of gaiety and celebration, not violence and discord. The city cheered the new governor, a neighbor. As Millard Fillmore Caldwell strode to the platform, he paused to note that exactly one hundred years earlier, Florida's first governor, William D. Moseley, addressed Floridians from the east steps of the Capitol. The new governor offered kind words to outgoing governor, Spessard Holland, thanking him for his "sound and solvent administration." The inaugural address was short and to the point; no one needed to be told they were amidst war. A wartime clause reminded Americans: "For the duration."

Governor Caldwell warned that the "trend toward centralization of government powers has progressed too far and must be curbed." The new governor also cautioned Floridians to prepare for new fiscal realities "because of a chaotic war, abnormal receipts from its taxes and subnormal expenditure of its funds . . . In seeking more revenue, we must avoid undue hardship. Confiscatory taxation will destroy the very foundation of the state." He also criticized the state's woeful educational system and emphasized the need to reform and improve its schools.[30]

Hidebound conservatives and traditionalists, Governors Holland and Caldwell faced a reckoning. Standing before a mirror prior to the inauguration, outgoing governor Spessard Holland detected the problem: He had gained thirty-five pounds since he last wore the guest suit four years earlier. "I have a time keeping the vest buttoned," he admitted. Meanwhile, the governor-elect did not like the custom of wearing a tall silk top hat, no matter the occasion. "I just don't like the idea one bit," he grumbled. "I'd much rather wear my plain old business bonnet." Ultimately, he yielded. "For tradition's sake, I'll wear the thing," he sighed.[31]

In a day filled with customs and propriety, former governor Holland and his wife Mary Agnes quickly departed the Capitol, bound for their beloved Bartow. But thousands remained, eager for the round of parties and balls. A formal reception took place at the Capitol Rotunda "for the citizens of Florida" who attended the inauguration. In the world of 1945, this meant that thousands of white Floridians celebrated the changing of the guard. The Capitol Rotunda, noted the local paper, "was attractively decorated . . . in a profusion of greenery." The Leon High school band provided the music. Tallahasseeans and guests flocked to the governor's mansion to greet the new First Family. The Camp Gordon Johnston band played festive music for the occasion. Celebrants also enjoyed two balls at the Florida State College for Women. The Dale Mabry Field orchestra played as the First Family welcomed friends and neighbors. A reporter noted that Mrs. Caldwell "wore an attractive black French gown with a three-pieced flounced skirt and a square neckline. On the left shoulder was a fuchsia bow."[32]

Governor Caldwell Takes Charge

Caldwell's reputation as a brusque administrator was quickly established. His first cabinet meeting was scheduled for ten o'clock. He canceled the meeting at 10:01 for lack of quorum. "Thereafter the cabinet met at ten o'clock sharp and we dispensed with the business," he recalled.[33]

Juanita Greene was a rarity in 1945: a female reporter who covered the news, not merely weddings and society events. Later, she became the *Miami Herald's* first environmental reporter, but in January 1945, she had recently been hired by the *Tampa Daily Times*, principally because so many male reporters had been drafted. Ordered by her editor to ask Governor Caldwell why his appointments to the Tampa Port Authority had snubbed some local "bigwigs," she dialed the governor's office.

A man's voice answered. "Could I please speak to Governor Caldwell?" she asked. "Speaking," the governor replied. When asked why he had not appointed more deserving candidates, he explained: "Young lady, in politics you reward your friends and punish your enemies. That is my explanation."[34]

The *Tampa Tribune's* J. A. Murray described the daunting task of appointing applicants to state boards and jobs. "The name of every applicant for every job, no matter what, is in a card file by the elbow of John T. Wiggington, his executive secretary . . . The file is a little shorter and fatter than a shoe box . . . On adjacent shelves are 10 similar files containing the names of thousands of Floridians, built up through weeks of work, arranged by counties." Wigginton succinctly summarized the system: "Brother, these tell the incoming governor where you stand."[35]

The new governor, alarmed by reports of indolence and all-night jook joints (unruly bars or taverns featuring a dance floor), sent telegrams to every Florida sheriff urging them to "use their good offices to eliminate idleness." As a bonus, the statute allowed sheriffs to keep all fines collected, up to $7,000 annually. Quickly, it became evident that wartime "Work-or-Fight" laws targeted African Americans. The sheriff of Martin County announced, "It is going to be the policy of this office to cooperate with farmers, saw-mill men, and others doing essential work to see that they get all the help available." Clearwater, according to a report, confronted "more than fifty chronic loafers, including some gigolos . . . Many were Negroes and borrowed money from their girlfriends to aid their loafing." Broward County Sheriff Walter Clark raided area slums and pressed African Americans, including some in uniform, to work on a farm owned by the Oakland Park mayor.[36]

Caldwell quickly faced the enormous administrative challenges confronting his governorship. A prisoner of the Florida State Constitution of 1885, the chief executive found himself checked and handicapped by an independent cabinet and a bewildering bureaucracy. The Democratic Redeemers, the Bourbon authors of the constitution whose memories of Radical Reconstruction burned deeply, dictated a weak chief executive.

Most importantly, the constitution forbade an elected governor from succeeding himself, meaning the inaugural ceremony marked day one of a lame duck. Cabinet members, however, could stay in office for decades. Voters elected and reelected Nathan Mayo as commissioner of agriculture for nearly four decades, 1923–1960.[37]

Attorney General Tom Watson posed a special problem for the new governor. Caldwell hired his own lawyers rather than deal with his prickly attorney general. Tom Watson "was my warm personal friend," reminisced the governor three decades later, but "was inclined to be erratic in his opinions and then inclined, without notice, to revise his opinion. . . . He was impossible as attorney general." Whereas Caldwell possessed the manners and demeanor of a courtly gentleman, Watson was a fiery, red-headed politician who lived up to his colorful nickname, "Fightin' Tom." A Virginian, he attended Virginia Military Institute, and following law school at Washington and Lee, enjoyed a successful practice in Tampa. In 1915, the thirty-year-old Watson became a city judge. State Representatives Watson and Caldwell had clashed before, as state legislators in 1931 over rural-urban issues. Audiences filled the chambers to hear Watson orate and, on occasion, engage in fisticuffs with spectators and colleagues. The following year, Watson ran for governor, the first of several unsuccessful campaigns. He was elected and reelected attorney general in 1940 and 1944.[38]

Watson and Caldwell clashed on many fronts, but they agreed on one issue: their hatred of labor unions. The wartime national emergency had catalyzed Florida's labor movement, as thousands of war workers, eager to secure union-wage jobs, flooded Tampa, Miami, Panama City, Pensacola, and Jacksonville. In 1941, Watson addressed an American Federation of Labor (AFL) convention, horrifying the audience by announcing, "I sincerely feel that the closed shop is undemocratic and un-American." Among union leaders, closed shop was exceedingly popular because it required all employees to belong to the union (effectively closing the door to those unsympathetic to unions). Watson also questioned the loyalty and patriotism of labor leaders in Tampa and Miami. In 1944, Floridians voted whether to ratify a constitutional amendment making Florida a "right-to-work" state, meaning that workers could not be compelled to join a union. Floridians adopted the anti-closed shop, making Florida and Arkansas America's first "right-to-work" states.[39]

For a generation, the Legislature had cobbled together balanced budgets dependent upon a rickety combination of gasoline and sin taxes, summed up in a popular jingle: "Bet, buy, die; Drive, drink, smoke." But Florida was emerging into a modern state, a much different place than a decade earlier. In 1934, the state's budget was $35 million; by 1944, it had exploded to over $117 million. Fiscal questions haunted legislators, mayors, and the chief executive. What will happen at war's end when Washington shutters hundreds of military bases and turns off the federal fiscal pump? Could Florida possibly manage growth and modernize public education without a state sales or income tax? Governor-elect Caldwell had confessed to reporters that the state's finances distressed him. Caldwell liked to call his fellow Floridians "stockholders." He would soon call the Florida legislature an insane asylum.[40]

Decades later, Caldwell was asked about the state of the state in January 1945. "The state institutions were poorly manned because so many of the personnel had gone to war, into war work . . . So when I was elected things were pretty well worn down."[41]

The 1945 Florida Legislature

The 1885 Constitution mandated that the Legislature meet every two years for sixty consecutive days. Wags suggested that Floridians would benefit more if the legislators met every sixty years for two days. Even more maddening to the new governor, the legislative body convened in April, leaving the chief executive little time to prepare. Governor Caldwell opened the 1945 session with an address emphasizing the need for ten to twelve million dollars in new funds needed for critical state services. "Short and to the point, it [speech] left little doubt as to the chief executive's legislative program," editorialized the *Palm Beach Post*. The *Ocala*

Star-Banner concluded, "While the message is factual and fiscal to a degree, it is to the point with no useless verbiage."[42]

The war had wreaked havoc with the state's budget. Gasoline rationing saved precious resources but reduced revenues. The federal government had permitted horse and dog racing during 1944, a policy resulting in $7 million into the state coffers. But Washington suspended racing track operations in 1945. Caldwell refused to consider proposals to legalize and tax general gambling, as well as ask for a sales tax or income tax. Rather, he persuaded legislators to increase the utility tax, levy three cents tax on a bottle of beer, twenty cents on a gallon of wine, add a penny tax on cigarettes, and hike dog racing and jai alai proceeds. Florida's taxes on gasoline, beer, liquor, and cigarettes were already the highest in the nation. The Legislature passed one noteworthy piece of legislation. For the first time in Florida history, state employees were eligible for a retirement pension.[43]

Political observer Allen Morris wrote that Spessard Holland, the previous governor, faced the same fiscal challenges as Caldwell. But Morris argued "that when Holland pulled those strings as governor, he could from having served eight years in the state senate . . ." Morris would not be the last to point out that while Holland had a strong relationship with legislators, Governor Caldwell seemed aloof and above the political fray.[44]

While many state newspapers urged the legislature to tackle the controversial issue of a new state constitution, the session seemed as if it would end harmoniously. On 27 May, Governor Caldwell declared that he expected the governing body "to observe the mandate of the constitution and perform its duty [of reapportionment]." On the first of June, Caldwell told the press that he was not prepared to "determine what reapportionment is in compliance with the constitution, but some reapportionment must be accomplished." Customarily, veteran legislators ignored the new governor. As the handkerchief floated to the floor at 4 o'clock on the sixtieth day of the 1945 Legislature, and as the temperature reached one hundred degrees, cracker accents bellowed "*Sine die!*" However, Caldwell dashed travel plans. The governor announced a call for an extraordinary session, the first since 1931. The session's charge was to consider a single issue: reapportionment. And the task would begin the next morning.[45]

In this era of biennial legislative sessions, most state senators and representatives worked for a living, practicing law or medicine, farming or managing family businesses. Considering that the State of Florida paid legislators six dollars a day during the extraordinary session, most were eager to leave town. But not everyone. George Nesmith, a self-described Crawfordville "seine yard operator and former saw miller," told a reporter, "The mullet don't start running in the Wakulla River until the tenth of October, and I'll sit here as long as you do."[46]

Cries for reapportionment rallied South Florida politicians who demanded fairness while North Florida and Panhandle leaders scoffed at the mere mention of change. The 1885 Constitution demanded reapportionment every ten years based upon population changes, but legislators had long ignored the mandate. Rapidly growing South Florida had become prisoner and poster child of the 1885 document. Newspaper editorials mirrored regional concerns. "We deplore the actions of those senators which has made necessary an extra and perhaps costly session," contended the *St. Petersburg Times*. The *Tallahassee Democrat* countered, "There are many arguments for and against reapportionment. One argument for it is based upon population being represented. One complaint against it is based upon the soundness that comes in government from representation of all sections." The *Fort Myers News-Press*, however, questioned Caldwell's motivation. "Unfortunately for the cause of just reapportionment of the state legislature there was little iron in Governor Caldwell's voice. . . . In fact, his message was almost apologetic."[47]

Remembered in political lore as "53 Days of Futility," the 1945 extraordinary session taxed and tested the patience and manners of the legislators who gathered during the steamy months of June and July. That historic occurrence was a distorted mirror, a battle between visions of what Florida was and should be, an inflection and reflection of 1945 politics and society.

A single Republican, Alex Akerman Jr. of Orlando, was the first of his party to serve in the State House of Representatives in almost two decades. His father had been nominated by President Calvin Coolidge to serve as a federal judge in Central Florida. His Orlando law firm earned a reputation for their steadfast dedication to justice for Floridians. Yet for all his accomplishments, Akerman, a war veteran, was seated only after a last-minute challenge whether to allow the lone Republican a seat in the House of Representatives. Few contemporaries could have imagined that decades later, historians would portray Akerman as a civil rights hero in a place few Floridians knew: Groveland. As a legislator, however, he was as inattentive as he was ineffective.[48]

No African Americans served in the 1945 legislature, although John Proctor, the last surviving African American member of the 1873 Florida Legislature, celebrated his hundredth birthday in 1945. Proctor's life encapsulated a century of Florida history: Born into freedom in antebellum Leon County, he was sold to pay the debts of his father. Following his legislative career, Proctor became superintendent of customs for the Port of St. Marks.[49]

The oldest member of the body was eighty-six-year-old Jefferson Alexander Hendley, who had been a member of the 1885 legislature that had "wrested the state from the carpetbaggers." The son of a Confederate surgeon, Hendley took pride that he had surveyed frontier Pasco County, and later wrote a history of the county. In 1945, he claimed the oldest diploma of any Floridian, having graduated from Washington and Lee University in 1878.[50]

The 1945 Florida Legislature included a single woman, a remarkable individual. First elected in 1943, Mary Lou Baker became only the second female to hold office in that body. A resident of St. Petersburg and Clearwater, she sponsored three pioneering bills involving women's rights. Most significantly, she spearheaded the Married Women's Rights Bill in 1943, popularly known as the Women's Emancipation Act. The bill gave women the right to manage their property separately, sue and be sued, convey property, and execute documents. Following the bill's passage, Miss Baker said simply,

"Isn't it grand?" Representative Baker, however, failed in 1943 and again in 1945, in her crusade to grant women the right to serve on juries. Her presence and cause provoked controversy. Rep. Warren G. Sanchez of Live Oak declared that the average mother should be "more concerned about her children at dinner time than about listening to testimony in a trial." Others depicted the bill as a Trojan horse, a devious way to open the door to black women voting. When running for reelection in 1944, Rep. Baker's "feminism" became a campaign issue. When questioned why she continued using her maiden name, the legislator calmly defused the issue. "The purpose of a name is to designate an individual, and to distinguish that individual from others . . . It might even be considered unsportsmanlike for me to use the name of my husband upon the ballot and thereby borrow from the goodwill established by the name of Captain Seale H. Matthews." A victorious Mary Lou Baker made a "most unusual post-campaign statement." She announced that she had just phoned her husband the joyous news that she was pregnant. In the 1945 session, Baker played a significant role in the debate over the future of the Florida State College for Women.[51]

Hundreds of legislators, secretaries, clerks, messengers, and janitors reluctantly shuffled into Florida's antiquated Capitol on 10 June 1945. Erected in 1845, the building had survived three additions, the most recent renovation in 1939. "In the pre-air conditioning yesteryears," reminisced Allen Morris, "the House Chamber, because of the wide-open windows to admit the breezes, served as the home for birds, to the dismay and hazard of the Representatives and others seated below the lighting fixtures which were roosting places." The Senate Chamber, reflective of its status, boasted a first-generation air conditioning system, which rarely worked. Visitors detected pandemonium. "There was the clatter of kicked spittoons and collapsing metal folding chairs," remembered Morris, "the hum of a hundred conversations, the shout of members trying in debate to make themselves heard. The open galleries contributed to the bedlam . . . a haze of tobacco smoke hung over the chamber . . . There was even the whimper of a dog that came with its master." Wartime shortages had even modified the landscape of the House and Senate floors. In support of the city's many salvage drives, Secretary of State Gray donated the rubber mats that once lined the spittoons.[52]

In 1945, Tallahassee was a small town of eighteen thousand inhabitants in a dry county with a black majority. The city came alive every other year. "There was a half-moon of rooming houses and boarding houses about the Capitol," recalled Allen Morris. "Nearly all the attachés [aides] lived in these." Legislators with families rented homes. Many legislators, lobbyists, and journalists stayed at Tallahassee's two most elegant hotels, the Floridan and the Cherokee. The Cherokee boasted "air-cooled rooms," recalled Vernon Peeples, who served as a thirteen-year-old page in the 1943 legislature. Peter Oliphant Knight, a corporate lawyer for Florida's most powerful companies, allegedly rented an entire floor at the Floridan, to "entertain" legislators. A veteran legislator recalled top-shelf whiskey being served at the Floridan's hospitality suite by young Cuban women, wearing only underwear. The Floridan's air-conditioned lobby was a rarity. Bernie Papy, the colorful Key West legislator, hosted an annual fête, serving green turtle soup to democrats and Democrats.[53]

Jacksonville's Ed Ball, a banking magnate, land baron, and trustee of the DuPont estate entertained legislators at his rustic lodge at Wakulla Springs and the Hangman's Hideout in Tallahassee. The Silver Slipper and Joe's also attracted free-spending crowds, in part, because private rooms and doors protected furtive behavior and, in part, because lobbyists picked up the tab. Legislators learned quickly which clubs—the Forest Inn, the Cotton Club, Capitol Gardens, the Edgewood Inn—featured black market steaks, liquor, and gambling. Entrepreneurs promised curbside delivery of premium brand liquor and bootleg hooch.[54]

The Battle over Reapportionment

The crazy-quilt political drama that unfolded in the summer of '45 sprawled across political, geographical, and legal borders. Reapportionment mattered so dearly because it respected the past, debated the present, and augured the future of Florida.

Between the founding of Pensacola and St. Augustine in the 1560s and 1940s, North Florida and the Panhandle had largely governed and dominated Florida. The reasons why compress nearly four hundred years of Florida history: the geo-political location of La Florida as a colonial bulwark against invading Protestants and sanctuary for Spanish ships; the choice of Tallahassee as the territorial and state capital; the Black Belt's riches; the population of Middle Florida; and the location of Florida State College for Women, Florida A&M College, and the University of Florida. Sidney Johnston Catts may have been the last politician elected governor (on the Prohibition ticket in 1916) by corralling the votes north of the Suwannee River, but the region continued to exercise disproportionate political influence for a half century. For most of the twentieth-century, North Floridians chaired the most powerful committees, commanded a disproportional number of senate presidencies and house speakerships, and held the most influential cabinet positions.

The pulse beat of Florida was no longer DeFuniak Springs and Lake City, Wauchula or Perry (the hometowns of Sunshine State governors between 1917 and 1941—Sidney Catts, Fred Cone, Doyle Carlton, and Cary Hardee), but Miami and Fort Lauderdale, West Palm Beach and Orlando, Tampa and St. Petersburg. The war years had introduced millions of soldiers, workers, and tourists to Florida. Many became residents, as the population of the Sunshine State spiraled from 1.9 million in 1940 to 2.3 million in 1945. Over 90 percent of these new residents settled in the fast-growing peninsula. "Senate reapportionment, in simple terms," editorialized the St. Petersburg Times, "means giving more senators to regions that have more people, taking senators away from regions that have few people."[55]

But sheer demographics and economics had not translated into political power. In 1945, Florida's five most populous counties (Dade, Duval, Hillsborough, Pinellas, and Polk) represented almost half of the state's residents yet claimed only 13 percent of the state senators. In the Florida House, each Dade County legislator represented 105,046 citizens, while the Glades County legislator represented 2,281. Hamilton County's 9,778 inhabitants had its own state senator, but John R. Beacham represented 119,783 residents in his combined Palm Beach and Broward counties district. The reason for malapportionment was simple: no previous Florida governor or legislative leader had forced the issue. To reapportion was to commit political suicide. "It is a mighty poor cat," explained Governor Catts, "that won't look out for its kittens." Robert Sikes, who replaced Millard Caldwell as a Panhandle congressman, spoke the language of the Yellow River code and the Panhandle: "The he-coon looked after those who depend upon him. Your word was your bond." He-coons also looked after their favorite sons and grandsons. In the 1940s, twelve of the twenty-two North Florida senators and representatives traced their lineage to former state legislators. Many legislators traced their political skills to their days at the University of Florida.[56]

Governor Caldwell may have shared a love for his region's red clay, white grits, and yellow pines with fellow statesmen, but they did not reciprocate the love. The North Florida bloc was furious that the governor had forced them to confront the unpardonable issue of reapportionment. Caldwell had not forgotten that only four members of the 1945 legislature supported his candidacy for governor. Most preferred Lex Green. Caldwell held the rule of law dearly, and his strict construction of the constitution concluded that the legislature had abandoned its duty. Caldwell was a stickler for rules and duty.[57]

In a 13 July 1955 *Tampa Tribune* editorial, James Clendinen coined the term "Pork Choppers" and "Pork Chop Gang" to describe the North Florida bloc whom, for decades, had fought "for pork rather than principle," in contrast to the more urbane "lamb choppers" of South Florida. If one expected pork choppers to slavver guilt for their conduct, one would be mistaken, if not delusional.[58]

Scott Dilworth Clarke epitomized the pork choppers. Clarke's father and uncle fought for the Confederacy; his grandfather gave his life for the Lost Cause. When Clarke was born in 1882, Republicans still ruled Jefferson County, a black majority county. As a student at Florida Military College in Bartow, Clarke felt the presence of Major General E.M. Law, a hero at the Battle of Chickamauga. The ambitious graduate returned to Jefferson County where he was elected mayor of Monticello in 1903 and to the Florida House of Representatives in 1907. For six decades, Clarke represented Jefferson County's four thousand whites and eight thousand blacks. Serving in the Florida Senate from 1930 to 1967, no one ever articulated the meaning of reapportionment better than Clarke. During a heated exchange over a motion ceding Liberty County to Clarke's Jefferson County senate district, Clarke pleaded famously, "If you give me Liberty, you give me death!" Decades after the infamous reapportionment struggle of 1945, a contemporary reduced the imbroglio to its simplest terms: "No one really wanted to upset the Judge!"[59]

The South Florida faction threatened to take the fight to the courts. Governor Caldwell expressed disappointment over "the litigation angle," believing that such threats "destroyed the harmony that was prevalent and growing." Such action was also considered quixotic since most of the judges had been appointed by Florida governors who supported the status quo.[60]

Insults also failed. Pinellas County Rep. S. Henry Harris depicted the opposition as "a damnable conspiracy conceived in the political greed and born under a live oak tree sharing its shade with a north Florida hog pen." Editorials in Tampa, Miami, and Fort Lauderdale papers eviscerated the North Florida opposition, logically pointing out the numerical and ethical unfairness. But each new bill that promised to address the inequities was squashed. "Gentlemen," Senator Amos Lewis of Marianna reminded his colleagues, "We are ready to kill your bill." Lewis, an astute leader, pointed out that the 1885 Constitution charged the Legislature with the power to reapportion districts based on population only so far "as practicable." Senator Newman C. Brackin, Okaloosa County, was even blunter, exclaiming, "I don't care what the constitution says . . . I'm fighting for power and control." Philosophically, Lewis's colleagues argued that apportionment should not be based merely upon population; rather, the dreams and interests of Jeffersonian yeoman farmers should also be calculated. The enigmatic Attorney General Tom Watson of Tampa waded into the debate by suggesting that the legislature discount population in place of "age, area, contiguity, historical background, and resources." Another legislator argued that pine trees, not merely people, also needed representation.[61]

"As the debate devolved into a siege," writes historian Kevin N. Klein, "the strength of the North Florida position became clear. They controlled at least 20 seats of the 38-member Senate." But the North Florida bloc began to buckle. A St. Augustine legislator proposed that North Florida cede one seat to the South. Senator Walter Fraser proposed that Hamilton County be the sacrificial lamb. It was no mere coincidence that Hamilton County's senator, J. Graham Black, was in a Valdosta, Georgia, hospital, during the debate. Tensions matched the rising temperatures. In a Tallahassee restaurant, Senators Ray Carroll of Kissimmee and Bert Riddle of Darlington engaged in a "slugfest." When he was not politicking and fighting, Senator Riddle served as a school principal and hymn writer. Meanwhile, due to the grave political debate, physicians removed Senator Black's oxygen mask, and an ambulance rushed him to Tallahassee to save his political life.[62]

Perhaps the most colorful legislator was Jackson County Rep. Wankard Pooser. For good reasons, Malcolm Johnson described Pooser as "a slayer of sacred cows . . . [who] blurted out truths about members and lobbyists . . . and looked and acted like a man whose name might be Wankard Pooser." He once so abused a fellow legislator that his wife, Maude Marie—the mother of his eleven children—insisted on sitting beside him to help curb his tongue. In a rare moment, Rep. Pooser apologized to the assembly in May 1945, stating, "I am withdrawing from politics for which I feel myself totally unfitted anyway." Pooser had gained notoriety for his single-minded pledge to vote no on every bill placed before him. His tombstone at Pope Cemetery in Sneads reads simply, "The one and only Wankard Pooser. She loved me too." Wankard Pooser notwithstanding, it was an era when citizens identified with and befriended their politicians.[63]

Eccentric characters and intemperate feuding notwithstanding, the summer session allowed an intimate peek at the public's attitude toward their members. During the extra-session, legislators received six dollars a day, scarcely adequate. In Broward County, merchants set out empty barrels, so customers could help their legislators. One sign in Fort Lauderdale read, "Your pennies, dimes, dollars will help fight North Florida stubbornness." A merchant beamed that over $500 had been raised. Two weeks later, reporters asked Broward representatives about the campaign, and they replied they "hadn't received a dime." A Fort Lauderdale businessman in charge of the operations promised the funds—all $850—would be wired immediately.[64]

If logic, morality, and threats could not resolve the political gridlock, South Florida leaders pressed for the ultimate solution: secession. Promptly, newspaper headlines announced a drive to create a forty-ninth state. "Our people perceive no present relief from intolerable sectionalism except in a movement for a secession of South Florida and the setting up herein of a new commonwealth," editorialized the *Belle Glade Herald*. Georgia Governor Ellis Arnold promised that the Peach State would gladly accept any sectional leftovers. The price? "Two 300-pound hogs and one good hound dog." The idea quickly died. However, legislators soon introduced another vexing issue: the relocation of the state capital to Orlando. That idea, too, evaporated. But not before the *Orlando Sentinel's* legendary publisher, Martin Anderson, responded by taking out a large advertisement in the *Tallahassee Democrat*. "Keep your state house. . . . We're doing other things in the Orlando territory. Keep your state capitol. Orlando doesn't want it . . . We are a friendly city of Florida. We are not scavengers, chiseling the payrolls of other towns. Keep the capitol in Tallahassee, but give us justice."[65]

Finally, after 113 days in combined sessions—a record—the ordeal ended in late July. When political leaders told the governor that they were deadlocked, Caldwell urged legislators to "abandon their positions and adamant disagreement." The compromise involved concessions to award North Florida a new senate seat and add three additional South Florida seats. Broward, Palm Beach, and Alachua counties finally had their own state senators. During the debate, Senator W. Turner Davis, the "Old Gray Fox" of Madison County, branded Senator William A. Shands (Alachua County) and co-conspirators "Judas Iscariots and Benedict Arnolds." While the North Florida majority was now preciously thin, one should consider that between 1947 and 1965, every Florida Senate president was a pork chopper.[66]

Governor Caldwell signed the bill but paid a price. One paper editorialized, "Governor Millard Caldwell . . . has been crucified by the frightened and angered west Florida senators and berated by some of the south Florida press because he won't club the west Floridians over the head and make them obey the constitution." The *Tampa Tribune* criticized the governor for "straddling the top rail of reapportionment fence . . . instead of taking a firm stand on this issue." Journalist Allen Morris summarized the "53 Days of Futility," noting, "Beneath a veneer of forgive-and-forget, of the grin of the good loser, senators of Florida have gone home cleft of ill-will." The *Tampa Tribune* shrugged, "The agony is over," adding, "We refuse to recognize the result, however, as a 'victory' for South Florida." Caldwell's assessment of the 1945 legislature was brutally honest: "They labored manfully for a couple of months and brought forth a mouse."[67]

For all the political pettiness and partisanship, a sense of perspective provides some insight onto Florida's summer of '45. Strikingly, the Legislature convened just prior to Allied victory in Europe and concluded on the eve of VJ (Victory over Japan) Day. The debates occurred largely without reference to the greatest event in their lives—a raging world at war. A *St. Petersburg Times* editorial captured the importance of the moment, labeling the conflict "a fight between the Florida of yesterday and the Florida of tomorrow."[68]

V-J Day: The End of the War

As legislators boarded trains and steered their Dodges, Pontiacs, and Buicks home on 25 July 1945, Floridians fully expected the bloody conflict in the Pacific to drag on for many months. In planning the invasion of

Japan, codenamed Operation Downfall, military leaders had circled 1 November as D-Day. Dramatically, the dropping of two atomic bombs in early August changed everything. On the tenth of August, Governor Caldwell issued a proclamation anticipating V-J Day: "WHEREAS, the solemnity and dignity of the occasion should urge that all liquor package stores, bars and tap rooms and other places dispensing alcoholic beverages, remain closed during that period." Three days later, Governor Caldwell sent a telegram urging President Harry Truman not to accept anything less than the unconditional surrender of Japan. The next day, Japan capitulated, marking the beginning of what arguably was Florida's wildest evening of boisterous celebration.[69]

The war had unleashed the Four Horsemen of the Apocalypse upon Europe and Asia, but despite the monstrous assaults against life and humanity, the conflict had boosted the fortunes of America and Florida. Across farm, field, and city, Florida was booming. But peace brought anxiety. Politicians pondered how many of Florida's nearly two hundred military installations would survive demobilization. The editor of the *Okaloosa News Journal* in Crestview reflected on the possibility of the closure of the massive Eglin Army Airfield: "What will we do after the war?" Congressman Bob Sikes had succeeded Caldwell as the Panhandle's "He-Coon." He observed, "My concern now was to protect the economy in my district."[70]

Not every community in Florida had the good fortune to have a congressman who sat on the Military Affairs Committee. The last months of war and first months of peace witnessed a furious scramble of base closings and hand-wringing. Floridians displayed creativity and vision repurposing abandoned military encampments. Sebring's Hendricks Field, which emerged as one of the first B-17 and B-29 combat training schools in the U.S., became Sebring Airport. Local promoters envisioned the paved runways as an attraction, and on 31 December 1950, the Sebring Grand Prix was born. The Marianna Army Airfield, declared surplus property, evolved to become a state tuberculosis hospital. Arcadia's Carlstrom and Dorr airfields were closed and revived as a mental hospital and prison. Colleges emerged atop abandoned runways and bombing ranges in Tampa, Boca Raton, Palm Beach, Opa-Locka, and Lake City. Tampa International Airport replaced Drew Army Airfield. At Leesburg, a German prisoner-of-war compound became the site for Lake Sumter Community College. The Richmond Naval Air Station, located twelve miles south of Miami, became Miami's Metro Zoo. Lakeland's Lodwick School of Aeronautics became the spring-training home of the Detroit Tigers.[71]

The story of Dodgertown is pure Floridiana and Americana. In 1942, the Navy selected Vero Beach in Indian County as a site to expand the municipal airport and create a training base. The $4.8 million Vero Beach Naval Air Station housed 2,700 marines and navy personnel and 300 WAVES. By June 1946, the base had closed. Vero Beach, a community of only 3,050 on the eve of Pearl Harbor, inherited the two-thousand-acre white elephant. In 1948, the Brooklyn Dodgers began searching for a more permanent spring-training facility in Florida. The team had spent previous springs in Sanford, Pensacola, Daytona Beach, Clearwater, and Orlando. Dodger's President Branch Rickey met with the mayor of Vero Beach and hammered out a sweetheart deal. The Brooklyn Dodgers took over the sprawling facility, paying one dollar a year to the city. For the shrewd Rickey, the deal was not only profitable, it allowed "the Mahatma" to integrate his team quietly and under the supportive cloak of Dodgertown and the small city of Vero Beach. On 12 December 1947, the *Vero Beach Press Journal* beamed, "Brooklyn Dodgers Select Vero Beach For Spring Training." Three months later, Governor Millard Caldwell displayed his athletic form by throwing out a first-pitch ceremonial strike.[72]

The decades following V-J Day unleashed a furious burst of consumer spending, buoyed by optimism and comfort knowing that among the war's combatants, only the United States was spared widespread bombing, the slaughter of civilians, and near-starvation conditions. When Americans returned from Europe and the Pacific, the GI Bill eased the transition and boosted the construction industry and higher education. Most significantly, Americans expressed soaring hopes and unbridled confidence in the future.

Peace ushered in a new Florida dream that captured the American imagination. Florida's beaches and cities had been introduced to two million homesick servicemen and women, most of whom vowed to return one day. And most did, as tourists, transplants, and retirees. The new dream promised inexpensive living amid a tropical setting flanked by palm trees and sand dunes to Americans looking for second or third chances and new starts. Luring senior citizens hoping to find the elusive Fountain of Youth, the dream hinted at possibilities of a better life. Among American states, California and Florida sparkled brightest as Sunbelt dream states.[73]

But for all the ballyhoo about the future, Florida was woefully lacking in advantages that presaged future prosperity. Unlike California, the Sunshine State's educational system, from kindergarten to universities, were second rate. Moreover, the state lacked modern industries relevant to the postwar world: aircraft, chemicals, and steel. The shipbuilding industry that had flourished during the war declined drastically after V-J Day.[74]

Most residents and politicians encouraged growth. Tempered by two decades of land busts and a Great Depression, Floridians now welcomed prosperity and the future. Good times meant more jobs, increased state revenues, and grateful voters. But growth brought new challenges: Yankee transplants from New York, Ohio, and Illinois, strains on the state budget, and bigger cities. Progress threatened a Southern way of life, and Caldwell was increasingly uncomfortable with changes to his beloved rural Florida.

The relief and optimism brought by the war's end did not translate into a harmonious first year in office for Millard Caldwell. The governor fully understood the upcoming challenges when in the hours after V-J Day, he remarked, "Peace is a crisis, and we may as well face the fact that rude changes are inevitable." A shift to a peacetime economy resulted in frustration and anger. Home builders complained about material shortages, housewives vented over food inflation, and African Americans raged about the irony of having fought to defeat racist dictatorships, only to return home to segregation and second-class citizenship.[75]

On the eve of V-J Day, the governor paused to ponder Florida's future. As Florida stood on the threshold of one of the most hopeful periods in

American history, the governor seemed preoccupied by the past, sounding more like the governor of the Magnolia State than the Sunshine State. Newspaper headlines read, "Governors Says Southern Way of Life Endangered." In a radio address, Caldwell warned Floridians of "highly organized movements steadily at work undermining the established way of life in the South." He also cautioned of movements "bent upon a new social order and a paternalistic form of government."[76]

Governor Caldwell was not alone in his anxiety over the future. On Thanksgiving Day 1945, Publisher John S. Knight of the *Miami Herald* wrote a gloomy editorial, citing a list of dispiriting developments that had descended over the world, including 200,000 striking General Motors workers, continuing violence in Palestine, Indonesia, and China, and starving children in Europe. Meanwhile, in Florida, "Race tracks are breaking all betting records, football stadiums are jammed to capacity, and amusement enterprises of all kinds reap a golden harvest. . . . [in an] orgy of escapism." The *Miami Herald* greeted 1946, editorializing, "A New Year begins today—a year that will be as fateful for the peace and progress of humanity as any in recorded history. . . . The challenge of 1946 to the United States of America for world leadership is staggering . . ." Senator Claude Pepper scribbled in his diary on 24 January 1946, "General Motors strike continues, steel strike on, meat strike in progress. . . . Russia has demanded Great Britain get out of Greece and Java."[77]

In April 1946, Governor Caldwell addressed a homecoming event in Sanford. He congratulated the veterans for their heroic deeds but cautioned that they may someday be "called upon to bear a heavier load." While American soldiers "saved this country from the alien hordes," he asked the crowd to help save America "from the domestic enemies of civic indifference, pacifism and selfishness." The governor also told Floridians to cinch their belts. "There is something in the present picture that disturbs me," he said. "We have thousands of unemployed veterans and former war workers already walking the streets."[78]

Caldwell's predecessor, Spessard Holland, addressed Florida's possibilities in more optimistic tones. In January 1946, Holland addressed the members of the Tampa Rotary Club. "Florida is the fastest-growing state in the Union," he announced. "A huge backlog of building, both public and private, awaits us . . . Savings deposits in banks throughout the state have reached unheard of levels." Holland went on to praise developments in the citrus and aviation industries.[79]

In September 1946, U.S. Senator Charles O. Andrews died. Like Holland and Caldwell, Andrews symbolized a Florida that was fast fading but still politically powerful. Born in Ponce de Leon, Florida, in 1877, a graduate of the Florida State Normal School in Gainesville, a Spanish-American War veteran, he ascended to the U.S Senate when Park Trammell died in office in 1936. Governor Millard Caldwell appointed Holland to the Senate, but not before offering Mrs. Andrews the opportunity to serve out her late husband's term. She declined. When Andrews had already announced that he would not seek renomination, Holland immediately pounced upon the opportunity and won the Democratic primary in May 1946. Governor Caldwell was pleased to appoint a fellow conservative and friend to the U.S. Senate. And fill Holland did, holding the seat until death in 1971. "It was a career that tagged Mr. Holland as a firm conservative," observed the *New York Times*, "opposed to most of the civil rights legislation that proliferated during his last years in office." [80]

Governors Caldwell and Holland, both participants in the Great War, welcomed the return of the newest generation of veterans. For aspiring politicians, membership in the American Legion or Veterans of Foreign Wars, was helpful if not essential. Future governors, Fuller Warren, Dan McCarty, LeRoy Collins, Farris Bryant, Hayden Burns, and Claude Kirk Jr. had all served in the military during the war. Reubin Askew enlisted as a paratrooper in 1946.[81]

Technological Mastery of Paradise

In 1513, on his historic voyage of exploration, Juan Ponce de León encountered a distinctive landmark along the coast of La Florida. He named the promontory "Cabo de las Corrientes" (tip of the currents). Navigators later named the area Cabo Cañaveral because of the dense canebrakes or reeds. It remains one of the oldest place-names in American history. The voyagers also encountered the Gulf Stream, a valuable discovery for Spanish mariners. The cape and its dangerous shoals posed a danger to vessels, and in 1838, the first of several lighthouses was erected on Cape Canaveral.[82]

As late as 1890, the population of Brevard County was sparsely settled, with 3,401 residents. In 1897, Millard Caldwell's birthyear, a collection of Harvard University graduates pooled their resources and acquired 18,000 acres, including several miles of Cape Canaveral ocean frontage. The Canaveral Club became a place where the Harvard graduates of the class of 1890 pursued the strenuous life, hunting and fishing during the winter season.[83]

In February 1946, a reporter for the *Tampa Tribune* toured the state, informing readers how change was sweeping across the peninsula. In Brevard County, J. A. Murray stumbled upon Canaveral, "a small community on the sparsely populated cape of scrub-covered key 14 miles or so to the northeastward of Cocoa." Canaveral had nothing "but a battered pier at which a busy shrimp fleet lands its catch." To reach Canaveral, one traveled a "worn old trail lost in the dense low-lying vegetation. . . . The place is remote and there are few signs of habitation."[84]

The Cold War settled into one of Florida's most unlikely places. Brevard County seemed serenely isolated from existential crises in Europe and Asia and the fast pace of Miami Beach and Fort Lauderdale. The combined populations of Cocoa Beach and Melbourne Beach in 1940 amounted to fewer than 150 residents. In 1946, Cocoa Beach employed one part-time police officer. The following year, the community acquired pipes and tiles from an abandoned war site and installed a water system. It was precisely Brevard County's remoteness that brought Cape Canaveral into the vortex of modernity. In 1947, the Joint Chiefs of Staff selected fifteen thousand acres around Cape Canaveral as a site for the Joint Long-Range Proving Ground. The site had been previously occupied by the Banana River Naval Air Station. Governor Caldwell enthusiastically approved and assisted the project that few could have imagined only a few years earlier.[85]

To critics, Florida's East Coast seemed a less than ideal place to launch rockets carrying dangerous fuel, given its setting for hurricanes, thunderstorms, and lightning. But in addition to Cape Canaveral's remoteness, the site's oceanfront location was ideal because rockets could crash into the open waters of the Atlantic without public or international consequences. Moreover, Cape Canaveral's nearness to the equator is ideal, allowing the National Aeronautics and Space Administration (NASA) to take advantage of the Earth's east-west natural rotation, giving rockets extra speed and efficiency.[86]

A vanguard of construction crews, engineers, and technicians arrived in 1948. On 20 July 1950, Florida's space age began with the firing of a 56-foot, 14-ton missile consisting of a German-built V-2 rocket with an American-developed WAC-Bumper in its nose. The missile roared over Cocoa at a speed of 2,700 mph. When asked what was happening to old Brevard County, a motel owner said simply, "We've all got rocket fever here."[87]

The transformation of Cape Canaveral from an isolated beach in a sparsely settled state and county to the apex of scientific research and technological advancements represents an important legacy of World War II. New words and terms accompanied such advancements: Aerospace, space race, jet age, rocket launches, and astronauts. From 16,042 inhabitants on the eve of Pearl Harbor, Brevard skyrocketed to 111,435 residents on the eve of JFK's New Frontier in 1960, and 230,000 residents on the eve of the *Apollo 11* moon shot.[88]

The struggle for paradise involved a battle to tame nature. The transformation of Cape Canaveral from an idyllic oasis to the space capital of the Free World was simply the most dramatic technological triumph in the heady postwar years when anything seemed possible—providing one had enough resources and will. In Florida, Isaiah's prophecies came true: hot became cold, the wet became dry, and earthbound mortals soared heavenward.

To Floridians and Americans, the war solidified the public's trust in technology and science. Peace promised that the same ingenious engineers that produced the B-29 Superfortress and the Jeep would duplicate their wizardry with homefront appliances and gadgets. Had not technology improved paradise?

The atomic age arrived on 6 August 1945. "Atomic energy is frightening to everyone," scribbled Claude Pepper in his diary. Few Floridians understood what exactly had occurred. Was an atomic bomb simply a very big bomb or something more sinister? Following Miami native Paul Tibbets's dropping the first atomic bomb on Hiroshima, Miami Beach Mayor Herbert A. Frink implored President Truman to hurl the weapon against nature itself—in this case an approaching hurricane. The Lee County Commission offered the U.S. government a 7,500-acre former military base, to be used for the "atomic bombing of hurricanes."[89]

To most Floridians in the late 1940s, air conditioning, not atomic energy, was the technology they wished to harness, Then, air conditioning was largely a luxury confined to large department stores and movie theaters. Floridians learned to make the best of hot, humid summers by adapting to nature, erecting wooden homes with ample windows. Most resort hotels closed doors in May, placards announcing, "Back in November." Given Millard Caldwell's fondness for the country, he most certainly would have agreed with his fellow Tennessean, Uncle Dave Macon. A popular performer on the Grand Ole Opry, Uncle Dave cracked, "I'd rather ride in a wagon and go to heaven than hell in an air-conditioned automobile."[90]

In 1943, the forty-one-year-old Miami writer Philip Wylie pondered a Florida unshackled by war. Worried about the future of his new home and city, he wrote a front-page story in the *Miami Herald*, knowing that a rush of new residents was about to flood his paradise: "Universal cheap air-conditioning after the war, plus the knowledge of tropical living we have gained during the war is going to end every problem of comfortable year-round living in south Florida." As V-J Day crowds descended upon Flagler Street in August 1945, the *Miami Herald* featured an article about the promise of new electric appliances. The manager of Richard's department store hoped that new air-conditioning equipment might soon arrive. The real breakthrough occurred in the 1950s, when the first inexpensive window air-conditioning units arrived. Still, as late as 1960, fewer than one in five homes in Florida had installed air-conditioning, but the revolution had begun.[91]

The widespread use of DDT made possible year-round living in remote and mosquito-infested barrier islands, as well as promising the eradication of palmetto bugs, cockroaches, and ticks. Most Floridians applauded the unrestrained use of DDT, for as the St. Augustine Record in 1945, "Aside from tax-dodgers and constant knockers, the mosquito is [Florida's] worst enemy." Engineers, scientists, and wizards also ushered in other modern breakthroughs, including air-conditioning, penicillin, Interstate highways, and bridge building.[92]

Technology relieved Floridians who could afford first-generation air conditioners. Air-conditioning also exposed class and racial distinctions. But in 1945, issues far more pressing and significant than air-cooled movie theaters loomed. Black leaders struggled for quality education, the right to vote, and peaceful coexistence.

Governor Caldwell and Race

African Americans had long known the harsh reality of inadequate housing, unequal schools, and stores bereft of quality goods. But such disappointments clashed with soaring hopes across postwar America. Victory over Imperial Japan and Nazi Germany validated American ideals as well as exposing fault lines. Black Floridians had supported the war effort and expected to be treated as full citizens in a new democracy. The decade of the 1940s was a heady time for black organizations in Florida. Thurgood Marshall, the pugnacious and indefatigable attorney for the NAACP, had already won several significant cases involving inequitable salaries paid to black teachers. Between the beginning and the end of the war, the number of NAACP branches in Florida doubled.[93]

A phalanx of black leaders focused on improving the lives of Florida's

African Americans in the postwar years. One such individual, Harry Tyson Moore, served as Florida field secretary for the National Association for the Advancement of Colored People (NAACP). His day job was teaching school in Brevard County. By 1946, Moore was concentrating his energies upon two issues: voting rights and police brutality. The U.S. Supreme Court decision *Smith v. Allwright* (1944) mandated that blacks could not be excluded from Democratic primaries. Energized by the court's decision, Moore helped organize the Progressive Voters League to register blacks, and his efforts bore fruit. In 1946, more than thirty thousand blacks voted in Florida's primaries; he ultimately registered one hundred thousand voters. Curiously, Brevard County officials refused Moore's request to register to vote. Resistance to Moore and his dreams ranged from the governor's mansion to Ku Klux Klan chapters to fields and groves.[94]

Moore's actions evoked outrage in Tallahassee. In 1946, an aide to Governor Caldwell wrote a county commissioner in Brevard County, inquiring "What about Harry T. Moore? He is a negro, is he not? Give me the dope on him." The commissioner replied tersely, "He is a troublemaker and negro organizer." Moore had begun organizing black citrus workers and registering voters: dangerous practices. He was also achieving success. "At the time of his death," cites his biographer, "31 percent of all eligible blacks in Florida were registered to vote. That was 50 percent higher than any other Southern state."[95]

Lynchings in Marianna and Live Oak in 1943 and 1944 had brought negative publicity to the Sunshine State, but nothing matched the outrage following the October 1945 lynching of Jesse Payne in rural Madison County. Lynchings had become increasingly rare—indeed, in 1930, a Florida newspaper headline read "Lynching To Be Lost Crime By 1940." Historian Tameka Bradley Hobbs observed that Caldwell "could not have imagined that the lynching of a black sharecropper in Madison County would haunt him for practically his entire term as governor."[96]

The only lynching in 1945 America, the Payne affair shocked the nation. What began as an argument over wages escalated to an accusation of raping a five-year-old child. Vigilantes snatched Payne, a sharecropper, from the Madison County jail and killed him. Governor Caldwell rejected the jury report that Payne had been "Shot with a Shotgun at the hands of Unknown Persons or Person." Dissatisfied with the jury report, Caldwell reluctantly launched a new investigation, asking Madison County Circuit Judge R. H. Rowe to impanel a grand jury to examine Payne's murder and the role of Sheriff J. B. Davis in the matter. The investigation revealed that keys had been used to enter the jail. Newspapers within and outside the state demanded the removal of the sheriff from office. But when a defiant grand jury exonerated Sheriff Davis, Governor Caldwell countered, maintaining that Payne's death "resulted from the stupid inefficiency of the sheriff and not from his abetting or participation." Sheriff Davis, insisted Caldwell, "has in this case proven his unfitness for office, [but] he was, nevertheless, the choice of the people of Madison County." The governor's statement ended with a quote that aroused national criticism and ridicule: "Stupidity and ineptitude are not sufficient grounds for the removal of an elected official by the Governor."[97]

The NAACP's Moore pummeled the governor for his mishandling of the Payne case and race relations in general. "This is the third time within the space of twenty-seven months that Florida's record has been marred by the brutal lynching of its helpless Negro citizens," he wrote to the Governor on 17 October 1945. "The better-thinking citizens of Florida will be grateful if you will take a firm stand in this matter."[98]

The governor ordered W. H. "Buddy" Gasque, a veteran investigator for the state attorney, to report on what had happened in Madison. In a confidential document, Gasque confided that "95% of the people were glad the lynching took place, and no one would give me any assistance." Gasque absolved the sheriff, pointing out that he had not assisted the lynch mob. Harry T. Moore called the governor's investigation "a farce." An aide to Caldwell admitted the "lynching of Negroes is really beginning to give the governor a headache."[99]

The more Caldwell attempted to parse the legal definition of lynching and place the events in the context of the South, the more the press ridiculed him. While many white Southerners may have approved of the governor's interpretation of events, most Americans were dumbfounded by his rhetoric and actions. Caldwell attempted to explain, "The ordeal of bringing a young and innocent victim of rape into open court and subjecting her to cross-examination could easily be as great an injury as the original crime. This fact probably accounts for a number of killings which might otherwise be avoided."[100]

From Caldwell's perspective, being shot and murdered in the South was not the same as being lynched and murdered. Caldwell insisted that Jesse Payne had been murdered, and the crime failed to meet the legal definition of a lynching. Caldwell's defense of lynching in 1945 sounded hauntingly like statements made in 1895 or 1915. But times had changed, even if many Southern governors had not. Southerners, he reasoned, understood the race issue and did not need meddlesome Northerners interfering in local and sectional affairs. He felt the furor following the Payne affair was simply another black herring determined to advance a federal anti-lynching law.[101]

Caldwell, when compared to other regional demagogues—Theodore "The Prince of the Peckerwoods" Bilbo and Eugene "The Wild Man from Sugar Creek" Talmadge—had enjoyed a positive reputation in the press. Now the Fourth Estate attacked the Florida governor and he counterattacked. When *Time* magazine criticized Caldwell over his handling of the Payne affair, the governor threatened a lawsuit, prompting an apology from publisher Henry R. Luce. When he read an advance copy of *Collier's* 23 February 1946 issue, Caldwell warned Henry La Cossitt, the magazine's editor, that the contents were libelous. "A Negro under indictment for attempted rape was snatched from jail and shot to death," *Collier's* contended. Caldwell insisted "that he didn't consider this a lynching. He went on to opine that the mob had saved the courts, etc., considerable time." In March, the governor's private counsel filed a half million dollar libel suit, pledging to donate any monetary awards to Florida A&M College, the state's only black four-year public educational institution. Florida's leading lawyers clashed inside and outside the courtroom. The jury awarded Caldwell $237,000. *Collier's* appealed the verdict, and in December 1948, a New Orleans appellate court reversed the case. A retrial was set at the federal courthouse in Gainesville. Jurors awarded Caldwell $100,000 in damages.[102]

The Payne affair damaged Governor Caldwell's image within and outside Florida. The Northern press lampooned an embattled Southern governor who refused to dismiss officials who seemed, at best, insensitive and incompetent; at worst, bigots. Florida's most prominent newspapers criticized Caldwell's handling of the Payne incident, branding the governor as stubborn, tone-deaf, and even embarrassing. Caldwell lashed back at the Fourth Estate and was especially critical of the *Tampa Tribune*. When Caldwell appeared at the annual Governor's Day luncheon held in Tampa, he castigated the hometown newspaper, remarking, "When I said there were no lynchings here, our Tampa press, sitting on its plush bottom, with self-righteous indignation, criticized me." Small-town papers, however, rallied around the popular governor. The Payne affair represented a test of wills and values in a changing postwar world. Millard Caldwell was a southern patrician who neither understood nor approved of a nascent civil rights movement and new sensibilities. He also believed that citizens deserved the candidates they elect.[103]

The governor defended his policy as "home rule," explaining that voters were responsible for removing derelict officials that they had chosen. "Do not expect the governor to correct your mistake," the governor maintained. "My theory was that as governor I was not elected chief of police." However, if the elected or appointed public official committed a crime, Caldwell was quick to remove the offender. Otherwise, Caldwell reminded the voters that they, not he, had elected the bumbling sheriff. Battered and embattled, the governor survived the Payne controversy, prepared to tackle even more formidable challenges.[104]

Historians have condemned Caldwell's role in the Payne lynching. Jack E. Davis contends the governor was more concerned how the news would affect Florida tourism. "Caldwell's semantic discourse was part of the South's attempt at that time to rid itself of an embarrassing tradition," writes Davis. Historian Tameka Bradley Hobbs deftly summarized,

"Caldwell seemed more annoyed than concerned by the Payne lynching." Ben Green describes Caldwell as a "stodgy conservative," who ignored the findings and recommendations of civil rights activist Harry T. Moore. Not only did authorities ignore Moore, but the Brevard County School Board fired him because of his activities.[105]

The governor was delighted to turn a new page as the 1945 calendar ended. On 3 January 1946, a newspaper assessed his one-year tenure: Governor Caldwell looked over the storm-spotted first year record of administration and reported that although "no goals" have been reached on the course he charted for Florida, the progress is "encouraging." At least he could take comfort in baseball not being politicized.[106]

New and Old Playing Fields

Racial strife was not limited to courtrooms. A new cause célèbre soon flared onto the front page when the Brooklyn Dodgers announced the signing of Jackie Robinson, a UCLA All-American athlete and a war veteran who had been court-martialed while stationed at Fort Hood, Texas. As a 2nd Lt., he refused to sit in the back of a military bus. In the words of Branch Rickey, the flinty president of the Brooklyn Dodgers, Robinson was "a race man," someone who maintained fierce pride of his color but who also understood that he was not to lash back at racists.[107]

When Robinson and his new bride Rachel arrived at Daytona Beach in February 1946, they discovered that baseball in Florida was both a reflection and refuge from reality. Floridians and Americans were giddy to hear "Play Ball!" Florida had not hosted spring training since 1941. But many Floridians were nervous, confused, and angry when they read in March 1946, "Baseball broke a long-standing precedent today when Shortstop Jackie Robinson and Pitcher John Wright, two Negro athletes, reported for spring training with the Montreal Royals." The fact that the American Communist Party sent a reporter to cover the events only reinforced suspicions. "Never before in this State or any other Southern State," informed the *New York Times*, "has a Negro played with whites in organized baseball . . ." Robinson somehow survived the spring of discontent, locked parks, and protests.[108]

Caldwell was relieved that the racial clouds hovering over spring training had dispersed, for the moment. Fulfilling an old campaign promise, the governor seized an issue guaranteed to revive approval ratings. When, he asked, would the University of Florida football team reward its long-suffering fans with a winning record? Fulfilling an old campaign promise, Caldwell demanded "a real football team" in Gainesville. He had approved an appropriation to build new athletic fields for the team, but warned, "As one fan, it won't satisfy me unless they produce a real team down there." He questioned whether the squad or coach had lost "either the ability to win or the ability to fight." The Gators' fortunes had fallen even below the mediocrity fans had come to expect. The Gator gridiron squad finished, alas, 0–9 in 1946.[109]

Nor was the postwar gridiron immune from race and politics. A dean at the University of Miami canceled a football game between Miami and Penn State, justifying his actions on "unfortunate incidents" that might occur if the Nittany Lions' "negro players participated."[110]

Ironically, the most significant football-related headline of 1946 was the hiring of A. S. "Jake" Gaither as head coach of the Florida A&M College for Negroes. As Florida A&M's acting head coach and athletic director, Gaither had been making $2,600 annually. As head coach, Gaither received a raise of one thousand dollars. Between 1950 and 1961, Gaither's teams won the Black College National Championship six times. Most Floridians were unaware of Florida A&M's successes because coverage occurred chiefly in the weekly "Negro page" of the larger urban daily papers, an issue delivered only in black neighborhoods.[111]

The newly created Florida State University (FSU) played its first football game on 18 October 1947, before 8,000 spectators. FSU reflected the integration of white men and women. The new team needed a proper nickname. In a hotly debated election, students preferred the nickname Seminoles over runners-up Rebels, Crackers, Tarpons, and Statesmen. In a banquet honoring the inaugural team, Governor Caldwell asserted that "the best football I saw played last season was by Florida State University," proving 'that top-rate football can be played on a non-commercial basis." Few future governors would describe college football in Florida as "non-commercial."[112]

Whether the issue was disappointment with the University of Florida football team or the issue of state's rights, Millard Caldwell offered his opinion with graceful prose and clarity of thought. In his Fourth of July radio address to Floridians, the governor maintained that Americans have surrendered "too much of our individual initiative and responsibility—too much of the vitally important sovereignty of the separate states."[113]

On rare occasions, Caldwell preferred indecision. In April 1946, the Junior Woman's Club of Miami invited the governor to speak on a proposed amendment to the federal constitution guaranteeing women equal rights with men. He confessed, "It may be the best policy for a mere man to stay on the sideline . . . and that is precisely what I have concluded to do."[114]

Education Reform: The Minimum Foundation Program

A resolute Governor Caldwell concentrated his energies in 1946 and 1947 on reforming Florida public education. He understood Floridians' frustration with an inadequate, even abysmal, educational system and informed Floridians in a rather frank approach: "You said you want good schools, and I want you to have them, but do not forget that you are going to have to pay for them." "Governor Spessard Holland had already appointed a blue-ribbon Florida Citizens Committee to study educational issues and suggest changes. Holland and Caldwell realized that businesses and residents demanded quality education for their workers and children. The challenges to reform such a vast bureaucracy was daunting. "As long as I can remember," Caldwell recalled, "candidates had promised better schools, better universities . . . No one ever did anything. I spoke roughly of the school situation and we got people angry enough to do something." Finally, a single question hovered above the fray: Could the governor convince citizens and the legislature to raise taxes to pay for the reforms? This question was especially pertinent because on the eve of the 1947 legislature, Florida's comptroller forecast a $9.7 million deficit if the legislature passed "the Citizens' state and local school bill."[115]

Governor Caldwell gathered a formidable team to inform and persuade politicians, educators, and citizens to advance reform. Newspaper editorials and research reinforced the committee's findings. No newspaper in the state tackled the issue with more zeal than the *Tampa Morning Tribune*. Arguably the state's most influential newspaper, with a daily circulation over 100,000, the *Tribune* assigned its top reporters to reveal the appalling conditions in the public schools. Beginning in 1946 and appearing almost every day for several years, the research exposed a failing educational bureaucracy. Even within some of the state's wealthiest counties, the quality of education varied greatly. Race, class, and geography mattered. Between 1946 and 1947, white teachers in the state's ten poorest counties earned a median salary of $1,493. Black teachers in those counties earned a median salary of $897. In the state's ten wealthiest counties, white teachers and black teachers earned respective median salaries of $2,243 and $1,802. Dade County, the richest in Florida, spent ten times as much for each student than Holmes County, the state's poorest. Compared to other states, especially postwar California, the Sunshine State fared miserably.[116]

Hillsborough County, home of the *Tampa Morning Tribune,* was a microcosm of Florida, a large county with rich and poor agricultural and urban areas. Students in middle-class neighborhoods received a superior education in clean and modern facilities. But in some of the rural and black schools, conditions were often appalling. The *Tribune's* graphic headlines revealed the plight: "Dover School an Example of Long, Pitiful Neglect," "Berry Schools Are Symbol of Sorry State of Affairs," "Pupils at Antioch Serve as Own Volunteer Janitors," and "Mango School Has All Evils of Neglect of Maintenance." At the Negro Industrial Home, Superintendent H.T. McCullough explained that to provide meat for the boys, "We go gopher hunting at least once a week." Voters elected county school superintendents, some of whom held office without a college degree.[117]

In January 1947, the Citizens Committee published its report, *Education and the Future of Florida*. Committee members recommended that the report be forwarded to legislators under the popular name, the Minimum Foundation Program. The recommendations included a minimum level of educational expenditures for every school district.[118]

In his address opening the 1947 Florida Legislature, Caldwell laid out his ambitious programs. He had spent time cultivating key legislators, including State Senator Scott D. Clarke of Monticello and Thomas D. Beasley of DeFuniak Springs, the new president of the senate and speaker of the house. Clarke had been a vocal critic of the governor, but a reporter found that "a campaign poster of Caldwell still hangs in his [Clarke's] back office at the old-timey Monticello bank." The governor hammered away on the point that unless the legislature provided ample revenue to finance the new programs, "teachers will be far worse off than they are now."[119]

A young, talented Tallahassee state senator played a crucial role in leading the fight to pass the Minimum Foundation Program. LeRoy Collins had vacated his senate seat in 1944 to enlist in the Navy, but not before serving as Ernest Graham's Leon County campaign manager in the gubernatorial race against his Tallahassee neighbor. Caldwell never forgave Collins for the slight, but Caldwell recognized talent and appreciated the senator's passion for education. "Though he was loathe to admit it later," writes Martin A. Dyckman, "Caldwell relied on Collins, who chaired the Education Committee, to overcome county resistance in the Senate. . . . Charley Johns of Bradford County, his future opponent, was the only senator who voted no."[120]

The Minimum Foundation Program modernized Florida's educational system. For the first time, the State contributed significant funds for school construction and operating expenses. In 1927, for example, the State Department of Education's footprint in Tallahassee was comprised of three rooms and one telephone in the Capitol building. The reforms greatly benefited the state's poorest school districts, ensuring that they could not fall below a certain minimum level. Furthermore, the legislation mandated a statewide nine-month school term. In years past, the length of the school term depended upon county budgets and political choices. Many teachers and school superintendents opposed the bill—at the time, only two of every three Florida teachers held college degrees—because salaries would depend upon educational qualifications. A delegation of North Florida legislators made a last-minute stand, appealing to teachers attending a Florida Education Convention in Tampa. They promised teachers a pay raise if they resisted the bill. But Caldwell threatened to veto any education bill that did not include the entire Minimum Foundation measures.[121]

Even though black leaders objected that no African Americans served on the Citizens Committee on Education, the Minimum Foundation Program benefited all Floridians. Two years after the implementation of the educational reforms, black teacher salaries increased to $2,616 per year, while white teachers were earning $3,030. Scholars argue that white leaders, aware of increased legal challenges by African American leaders and the courts, invested significant funds to make black schools appear more "equal" to white schools. "The states can't ignore the law of the land, and it looks as though more and more equality in education is going to be demanded," wrote Claude A. Barnett, director of the Associated Negro Press in a prophetic 1948 letter to Governor Caldwell. But most black leaders in 1947 Florida simply sought dignity and equality *within* Florida's segregated society. Legislators assured nervous white Floridians by changing the method of electing county school board members. For four decades, members had been elected by district. In 1947, precisely when African Americans began voting in Florida primaries, state legislators changed school board and county commission elections to an at-large format. Winning at-large elections at the county level posed a much greater challenge to African American candidates.[122]

The GI Bill and Higher Education

The year 1947 shook up the state of higher education. Reborn in the aftermath of WWII, Florida's higher education system was ill-prepared for the rush of veterans. In 1947, the Sunshine State did not have a four-year public institution of higher education south of Gainesville, and no comparable black school south of Tallahassee.

From a prewar peak of 3,456 students, the University of Florida swelled to 7,500 by the fall of 1946, as veterans enrolled, prepared for a new chapter in their lives. Describing the University's 1946 homecoming, an alumnus-journalist observed, "Gainesville is jammed from attic to basement." The reporter prepared alumni for a cultural shock. Student attire consisted largely "of one T-shirt," which he patiently explained was a "short-sleeved white athletic pullover."[123]

From its origins as East Florida Seminary and Florida Agricultural University in the nineteenth century to its emergence as the University of Florida in 1905, the school had functioned as a bastion of masculinity. Southern traditions and legions of Gator alumni in the state Legislature—and many of their wives—preferred that male and female students be separated: the former at Gainesville and the latter at Florida State College (FSCW) for Women in Tallahassee.[124]

New pressures eroded ivied walls and male sanctuaries. In 1945, Florida legislators passed a bill permitting student wives of discharged servicemen to attend the University of Florida. Angry that the state could not accommodate every male veteran seeking space in Florida classrooms, politicians petitioned FSCW president Doak S. Campbell to admit men. Governor Caldwell and President Campbell met frequently to discuss the present and future of FSCW. Caldwell's sister, a musician, had befriended Campbell, a chemistry professor, when they were young colleagues teaching at Central College in Conway, Arkansas.[125]

Caldwell greatly admired President Campbell and the two men worked together to implement the Southern Regional Education Board. They agreed to allow a few hundred veterans to enroll; however, Attorney General Tom Watson blocked the move. "We had no right, no legal right to put men students at Tallahassee," admitted Caldwell. "But we [Caldwell and Campbell] circumvented the problem quite well." The duo outmaneuvered Watson by establishing a "branch" campus of the University of Florida at Tallahassee. More than five hundred veterans enrolled, housed in barracks of the former Dale Mabry Airfield. "I came to the Tallahassee Branch of the University of Florida at eighteen," reminisced J. Earle Bowden, a native of Altha. He recalled living in the former Army Corps barracks at Dale Mabry Field, then known as West Campus "with veterans in Army khaki, Navy dungarees, paratroop boots, talking about the Big War with rowdiness frustrating the dean of men." But he remembered with fondness, "Across Tallahassee's hills, reachable by a fleet of buses, was an intellectual bastion of womanhood." Married couples lived in barracks-turned-apartments called Whispering Pines, popularly known as the "Fertile Crescent."[126]

Drastic action was necessary to avoid veterans expressing their frustrations at the ballot. Few politicians wished to confront legions of unemployed veterans. Higher education served as a social safety valve, becoming one of the most revered programs in American history. The GI Bill resulted in a rush of new students to Florida schools. Almost 8,500 men hoped to enter the University of Florida in 1946, but the campus could accommodate only 6,200 students. The solution, legislators and educators believed, was coeducation. Many FSCW alumnae resisted tampering with the university's traditions and its commitment to the liberal arts, but on 15 May 1947, Governor Caldwell signed pathbreaking legislation. Florida State University was borne out of war, politics, and necessity. The legislation also transformed the University of Florida into a coeducational school. In 1945, Florida's three public universities enrolled 7,000 students; by 1950, the number had increased to 19,000.[127]

Florida A&M began as the State Normal & Industrial College for Colored Students and opened its doors to students in 1887. In 1909, the name was changed to Florida Agriculture & Mechanical College for Negroes. Strikingly, when compared to other southern states, Florida stands out as having funded a single black public university. Male and female African American veterans flocked to Florida A&M.

In 1944, William H. Gray became the new president of Florida A&M College, having survived a scandal at Florida Normal & Industrial School

in St. Augustine. Zora Neale Hurston wrote Walter White, executive secretary of the NAACP in November 1942, beginning her letter, "Well, the
Negroes have been bitched again!" Hurston described Gray as "an insignif-
icant squirt," accusing the president and his wife of cheating young black
recruits at an Army Signal Corps facility at the college.[128]

After leaving Congress because of "creeping socialism," Governor
Caldwell now confronted an insurgent federal government that touched
Floridians' lives from cradle to school, from field to grave. As a strict con-
structionist, Caldwell abhorred federal dollars tied to low-income housing projects, the price of hogs, orange juice concentrate, and even school
lunches. Caldwell liked to point out that the word "education" is never
mentioned in the U.S. Constitution, but after Pearl Harbor, the presence
of khaki and federal dollars on campuses meant only one thing: "You're in
the Army now!" By 1946, the federal government was subsidizing Florida's
school lunch program with $1.1 million a year. Attorney General Watson
labeled the pact "state subservience," but the governor accepted the funds.
Like many conservatives, Caldwell may have complained, but nonetheless
fed at the federal trough.[129]

The GI Bill generated record numbers of undergraduates. But many
veterans also wished to enroll as graduate students in Florida. Such demand exposed fiscal and racial realities. Florida had not yet established
a single medical, dental, or veterinary school. Moreover, no law school
for African Americans existed within the state. Southern governors
met to discuss how their respective states might cooperate and share
the cost of graduate education. They met at a modern sanctuary of the
Old South—Ed Ball's estate at Wakulla Springs. They were determined
to modernize historically inadequate educational systems *and* resist integration, at all costs. Despite such rhetoric, Arkansas, Texas, Kentucky,
Virginia, and North Carolina admitted black medical students at public
schools.[130]

Among Southern governors, Governor Caldwell became the key leader
in the interstate education movement. In 1947, a compact was approved,
allowing southern white and black students to attend designated gradu-

ate programs. The NAACP had launched a series of lawsuits challenging segregated graduate schools. The U.S. Supreme Court ruled in *Sipuel v. Board of Regents of the University of Oklahoma* (1948) that African Americans deserved higher educational opportunities equal to those offered white students. The southern regional compact engineered by Caldwell maintained segregation while buying time from future court challenges. Caldwell frequently pointed out to "northern reformers" that southern schools (Meharry in Nashville and Howard in Washington, DC) enrolled more than a thousand black medical students, as opposed to a handful of comparable students in the "enlightened North." Under Caldwell's direction, the Southern Regional Education Board (SREB) considered taking over Meharry Medical College. Governor Caldwell testified before a Senate judicial committee, lamenting that "political and racial questions have been injected into" the issue of regional education. John Ivey, a sociology graduate student at the University of North Carolina in the 1940s and later a professor and official at the SREB, recollected that Caldwell, as opposed to contemporaries (Mississippi's Fielding Wright and Arkansas's Ben Laney) "wasn't an ideological racist. . . . The fact he was more of a pragmatic politician who wanted to get his program through made it possible for him to see SREB as an instrument for improving education in the South . . ."[131]

Passing educational reform was one challenge; persuading conservative legislators and Floridians to pay for the new programs was another. The governor asked legislators to consider raising $34 million in new taxes, to no avail. Conservative businessmen supported Caldwell's candidacy in 1944, but the victorious governor rejected a state sales tax, which he decried as inequitable. Ultimately, legislators and the governor kicked the fiscal can to the next governor and legislature.[132]

"There's Gambling in Florida!"

For solons and reporters, 1947–48 may have been the most intriguing, if not important, years in Florida political history. What Tallahassee may have lacked in urban amenities, the session more than made up with a memorable melodrama involving a sensational charge of bribery against a powerful legislative member.

Amid animated debate over the HB 590, first-term Rep. Brailey Odham (Seminole County) announced that he had been offered a bribe if he simply voted no. The press colloquially called HB 5990 the "anti-bookie bill." For decades, illegal gambling had flourished in Florida. Hillsborough, Broward, and Dade counties were home to gaming clubs, which the local sheriff and deputies allowed to remain open. But reports of slot machines near the state's military bases alarmed legislators. Advocates of the "anti-bookie" bill argued that the legislation would "cripple off-track bookmaking operations" that profited from the legal horse and dog tracks. Opponents of the bill argued, curiously, that the most effective strategy in stopping off-track betting would be to prohibit print and radio broadcast of race results.[133]

Odham, who at age twenty-seven was the youngest member of the State house, claimed he had been offered $200 by Rep. Bernie Papy, "the King of the Florida Keys," to vote the right way. Papy happened to be the most senior member of the House. Papy was well known for his green turtle soup and oft-quoted motto, "Always working for the best interest of Monroe County." Papy could be very persuasive. Odham testified that the accused had approached him the day before the vote and increased the offer: "I'll make it five [$500] and a case of Scotch whiskey if you'll just take a walk." Another member of the House also confirmed that he, too, had been approached by Papy. The legislative body asked a grand jury to review charges.[134]

Not since an African American representative was dismissed during the Reconstruction era had a House member been expelled for bribery. Papy, who had earned the reputation as a wealthy playboy, depicted his accuser as naïve and unaccustomed to the tradition of "old-fashioned horse trading." Papy hired legendary Tampa attorney Pat Whitaker to argue his case before the Grand Jury. The State Attorney branded Whitaker as "one of the most cunning criminal lawyers in the state." On the other hand,

Whitaker described Rep. Odham as a "baby legislator from Seminole County" and a dreamy reformer. The *Miami Herald* described the trial as one "of the most dramatic scandals in Florida history." The affair amplified the growing concern over organized gambling. Several county sheriffs, implicated in associations with gamblers, had been removed from office. The Grand Jury met for thirty-five minutes and acquitted Papy of all three charges of bribery. Undaunted and unbowed, the Key West powerbroker served another fifteen years in the Legislature. In 1965, his son Rep. Bernie Papy Jr. introduced a bill punishing scofflaws who advertised Key Lime pie not made with genuine Key Limes.[135]

Whether in the neighborhood barbershop or knelt in prayer, Citizen Caldwell sounded like a Baptist minister when the subject of illegal gambling was broached. But as governor, Caldwell refused to play the role of Archangel Michael casting out the demons to restore the moral order. In 1945, when five key witnesses testified in a Miami grand jury that Sheriff "Smiling Jimmy" Sullivan was corrupt while gambling was rampant on the Gold Coast, Caldwell replied, "I was not elected as a policeman. Control of gambling is a police problem." Although Bernard Papy had opposed Caldwell's candidacy in 1944, the governor remained aloof during the Papy scandal.[136]

Neither the governor nor many local officials cracked down on gamblers or gambling in Florida. If there was one city that gambling had flourished longer and more profitably than any other, Tampa deserved the honor. Cuban immigrants in the 1880s had brought the pastime game of *bolita* (literally, little ball in Spanish), originally associated with the Cuban lottery. Bolita grew in stature and power as Ybor City became one of Florida's most important industrial centers. By the 1940s, bolita had become a multimillion dollar industry, a business that had acquired political protection from local and state interference. Only when competition between rivals resulted in gangland slayings and unsavory public relations did locals attempt to control the "industry." In 1950, U.S. Senator Estes Kefauver of Tennessee, anticipating a run for the presidency two years later, seized upon a front-page story: organized crime in America. The organized crime hearings, a premier for the new medium of television, embarrassed state leaders and officials when it was revealed that Tampa and South Florida were centers of illegal gambling and mob corruption.[137]

The White Primary's Last Stand

On the volatile question whether African Americans should be allowed to vote in the primaries and register as members of the Democratic Party, Southerners scrambled to devise new plans and strategies to defy the U.S. Supreme Court. Governor Caldwell's defense of the white primary was simple: "I look at the primary as being similar to a club, adding, "I feel in the primaries each party has the right to determine its own membership." But the U.S. Supreme Court decision, *Smith v. Allwright* (1944) was the law of the land, however unpopular in the South. Only the liberal-leaning *St. Petersburg Times* editorialized in favor of the U.S. Supreme Court decision. "This is a fundamental right which cannot be legally denied to any citizen," the paper pleaded in 1945.[138]

In a desperate charge to stave off the implementation of the Supreme Court decision, Caldwell conjured up the ghosts of Reconstruction and promised resistance. In a November "no holds barred" interview with one-hundred members of the Florida press, he was asked about South Carolina's efforts to disfranchise blacks by placing the Democratic Party primary solely in the hands of the Party. "The South Carolina plan has considerable merit," the governor opined. Yet for all of Caldwell's stonewalling, the 1947 Florida Legislature distinguished itself from Deep South neighbors by its moderated response to the voting crisis. The Florida Supreme Court's decision, *Davis v. State ex. Rel. Cromwell,* 156 Fla. 181, So. 2nd 85 (1945), affirmed the rights of blacks to register as Democrats. In the 1947 Florida Legislature, Jacksonville Senator John E. Mathews Sr. urged fellow legislators to repeal all state election laws and follow the Gamecock State. But his fellow senators agreed with Secretary of State R. A. Gray, who insisted that a repeal of primary laws would result in massive voting fraud.[139]

In the end, state senators rejected the idea of establishing a private Democratic Party to run its primaries, voting 31–4 against Mathews's bill. In 1947, 13 percent of Florida's voting-age African Americans had registered to vote, in contrast to 4 percent in Mississippi, 5 percent in Alabama, 13 percent in South Carolina, and 20 percent in Georgia. By 1952, the percentage of Florida's black registered voters had climbed to 33 percent, the highest in the South. Harry T. Moore besieged the Department of Justice with letters complaining of Governor Caldwell's unwillingness to protect black voters in rural counties.[140]

Everglades National Park

The capstone to Florida's 1947 Legislature was the creation of the Everglades National Park. For decades, environmentalists and conservationists had fought to save the Everglades. In timely fashion, Marjory Stoneman Douglas's *The Everglades: River of Grass* was published in 1947. In a rare show of unity, moderates and conservatives helped bring the long-sought dream to reality, appropriating two million dollars to purchase land. But the preservation of the Everglades meant different things to supporters. To Governors Holland and Caldwell, the park saved the Everglades for economic and recreational development. They cared little about the environmental merits. "Holland," argues Michael Grunwald, "saw the park as a new way to convert swampland into prosperity." Florida's attorney general held up the project, arguing that the donation of state land and money was unconstitutional. Governor Caldwell once again outmaneuvered Tom Watson. On 6 December 1947 President Harry Truman formally dedicated Everglades National Park.[141]

The Everglades National Park's timing was inauspicious. The years 1947 and 1948 coincided with record rainfall and a major hurricane, saturating South Florida. The storms inflicted nearly $59 million in damages. Small farmers were just beginning to plant and harvest sugar in and around the Everglades. At the very moment the public celebrated the new national park, planters, politicians, and bureaucrats began to engineer the Everglades. In his magisterial biography of Marjory Stoneman Douglas, Jack E. Davis studied how the Army Corps of Engineers redesigned the Everglades. "Whatever its failed projects," writes Davis, "the Corps retained a rock-solid belief in its capacity to make water behave in ways beneficial to society."[142]

"It will be days, perhaps even months," editorialized the *Tampa Tribune*, "before citizens of Florida can gain a clear idea how the acts, and the failures to act, of the 1947 Legislature will affect their fortunes." Governor Caldwell and legislators received high marks for education reform, but questions remained as to the fiscal state of the state. Indeed, the next legislature faced mounting deficits and with great gnashing of teeth, passed the dreaded state sales tax. Editorials lauded the 1947 Legislature's creation of the Everglades National Park, while approving the "beating down" of the white primary proposals.[143]

3

THE WILD RIDE

Florida at the Crossroads, 1948

Few years have unleashed such whirlwinds. Everywhere, political ideologies swirled and collided. Old and new demons dominated the political conversation. The melodramatic political conventions pulsated to a climactic November ending.

In 1948, the aftershocks of WWII continued to reverberate. International events became intertwined with state and local concerns. A bloody civil war in Greece roiled the bayous of Tarpon Springs. In February, Maj. Gen. James Van Fleet was named chief of the American military mission in Greece. Van Fleet, a Bartow boyhood friend of Spessard Holland, coached the University of Florida football team, 1921–24, compiling the winningest record of any past or future Gator coach. Van Fleet served as the adviser to the Greek government battling the Communists. In Masaryktown, Oviedo, and Slavia, Florida, Slovak farmers openly wept at the news of a Communist seizure of power of Czechoslovakia. In Ybor City, the State Department urged Italians to write relatives in the old country to reject the Communist party. Tampa Spaniards knew letters were futile to impoverished and defeated relatives in Asturias and Galicia, since Generalissimo Francisco Franco and the nationalists won that terrible civil war a decade earlier. A *Tampa Tribune* headline announced, "Cuban Politicians in Exile Campaign from Miami Beach." *Time* magazine introduced the recently ousted Fulgencio Batista

Photograph of Governor Millard Caldwell in the late 1940s delivering speech in Sanford. Photo by Raymond Studio. Courtesy of State Archives of Florida, Florida Memory. https://www.floridamemory.com/items/show/133630.

as the "Senator from Daytona." On May 14, Jews across Florida cheered as Israel proclaimed itself a state.[1]

President Harry Truman seemed overwhelmed and overmatched by the sheer weight of issues and voters' memories of FDR. Truman's favorability ratings plunged to 40 percent in the 1946 midterm elections. In 1946, the Republicans had swept the national slate so convincingly, claiming 54 new Congressional and 11 U.S. Senate seats, that analysts evoked the word "realignment." The GOP's campaign slogan was simple: "Had Enough?"[2]

The issue of race continued to agitate the once Solid South. President Truman calculated he needed to win over northern black votes, even if it meant alienating southern whites. He appointed a controversial Committee on Civil Rights. The committee's recommendations challenged the sacrosanct doctrine of white supremacy, condemned segregation, criticized police brutality, and recommended the integration of the armed services. A Jacksonville Baptist warned Truman, "If that report is carried out, you won't be elected dogcatcher in 1948." The chairman of Florida's Democratic Party stated, "No sensible citizen can honestly support the president's plan to abolish racial segregation." The Florida State Association of County Commissioners denounced Truman's policies as "obnoxious, repugnant, odious, detestable, loathsome, repulsive, revolting, and humiliating to all true Democrats." Truman exacerbated the situation, if that was possible, when he issued an executive order integrating the armed forces. A letter signed "an ex-supporter and voter" informed the president, "If you think you're going to cram niggers down the throats of Southerners, you are badly mistaken."[3]

White southerners were dumbfounded by President Truman's views on race. A Missourian whose mother would not sleep in the Lincoln bedroom because of her bitter memories of a long-ago war not forgotten, Truman may have been an unlikely occupant of the White House, but he was determined to lead and passionately believed in the American Republic. He carried a copy of the Constitution in his suit breast pocket. Truman's idealism coexisted with his willingness to play political hardball. Truman realized the black vote in several Midwestern states might well determine the 1948 election. When asked how the civil rights furor might affect the southern white vote, his advisor Clark Clifford answered with an air of confidence, "As always, the South can be considered safely Democratic." Florida's Democratic delegates gave Clifford reason to reconsider, voting twenty to zero against the party's civil rights platform.[4]

Caldwell left no doubt his views on the vexing question of race and the South. On 16 April 1948, he broadcast a statewide radio speech, "The South and Civil Rights." He began in typical fashion: "Let us speak very clearly and very frankly about this matter of so-called civil rights." He barreled forward:

> Let those who advocate the adoption of laws creating a federal police system to enforce drastic punitive measures at the South honestly admit that they advocate a change in our form of government. Let them admit that, by the establishment of a Washington Gestapo to police the internal affairs of the several States, we depart from the ideals and concepts of those who founded this nation. . . . Florida would never presume to dictate to Georgia.[5]

Truman's worst nightmare occurred during the summer of 1948. In rapid succession, two vital wings of the Democratic Party—the Deep South and the liberal left wing—bolted to form third party challenges to the Democracy. South Carolina Governor Strom Thurmond burst on the national scene as the presidential candidate of the States' Rights Party, popularly called the Dixiecrats. Thurmond considered Caldwell a fellow crusader against federalism and civil rights, fully expecting the governor's support.[6]

In February 1948, Caldwell hosted the Southern Governors' Conference at Ed Ball's Wakulla Springs Hotel. Several governors, notably Mississippi's Fielding Wright, threatened "an all-out fight" to resist the president's civil rights agenda. While holding firm on the issues of states' rights and segregation, Caldwell and Tennessee governor James N. McCord emphasized that a schism in the party would surely result in a Republican triumph.[7]

Ingloriously dumped in 1944 from the Democratic ticket, the enigmatic vice president Henry Wallace became soul and symbol of the Democratic Party's left wing. Claude Pepper, hearing Wallace testify at a hearing, wrote in his diary, "Wallace magnificent on stand for himself. Only the President could have made a better statement of American progressive democracy." But Wallace also became a lightning rod because of his idealistic efforts at rapprochement with the Soviet Union and Joseph Stalin. In Pepper's same diary entry, he scribbled, "The reactionaries squirm, how they hate him!" Increasingly aware of the public's disaffection for the Republican and Democratic parties, Wallace felt empowered to act. A modern Don Quixote, he announced he would run as a third-party candidate. In March 1948, President Truman stated bluntly, "I do not want and will not accept the political support of Henry Wallace and his Communists. If joining them or permitting them to join me is the price of victory, I recommend defeat."[8]

The Progressive Party met in Philadelphia in late July 1948 to nominate Wallace. From the first moments of the convention that highlighted New York Congressman Vito Marcantonio, a suspected Communist, the press ridiculed the efforts of the delegates. When Wallace campaigned in the South, the hoarse crowds became coarse. "That renowned hospitality of the South," anticipated the *Miami Herald,* "is about to get its severest test since Sherman marched to the sea." On the stump, Wallace's presence inflamed Southerners, who upon one occasion hurled rotten eggs at the candidate. In North Carolina, Wallace famously placed his hands upon an elderly Southerner, asking "Am I in the United States?" The man responded, "Take your damned hands off-a-me."[9]

But in the Tampa neighborhoods of West Tampa and Ybor City, Wallace received a fulsome welcome. These neighborhoods, famous for their predominant Latin (Cuban, Spanish, and Italian) populations, had a history of fighting for progressive causes. In February, the candidate appeared at "*El Paraiso,*" the nickname of the Perfecto-García cigar factory. When Wallace addressed an integrated rally at Plant Field, elderly Latin cigar makers greeted the visitor with cheers of "*¡Viva Wallace!*" Residents never forgot

Wallace's support for the Republican cause during the Spanish Civil War. The son of leftist Spanish parents, Henry Wallace Lavandera was named for the progressive icon. "The strangest sight of all was the mingling of white and negro people in the grandstands," observed a reporter, a concession to Wallace and Tampeños. On 25 October, the African American baritone, movie star, and suspected communist, Paul Robeson, stumped for the Progressive Party in Tampa.[10]

In Tampa, not everyone cheered Wallace or his supporters. Letters to the editors of the local papers branded him "a disloyal member of the American family of freedom because he is backed by the Communist Party." The American Federation of Labor (AFL) also denounced Wallace. Denunciations of the integrated crowds sprinkled the newspapers and airwaves.[11]

One voice was particularly shrill and defamatory, urging Tampans to crush the seditious Henry Wallace. Maj. Gen. Sumter de Leon Lowry would not be stilled by a "former vice president" who "has been adopted as a leader by a party made up of enemies of our country." He added, "Communists are agents of Russia and Russia is our enemy."[12]

Like his nemesis Henry Wallace, Sumter Lowry was heir to a prestigious family. Born in the shadow of El Castillo in St. Augustine in 1893, he spent the rest of his life dedicated to becoming a citizen-soldier. A graduate of Virginia Military Institute, he returned to Tampa in 1914 to organize Company H, 2nd Florida Infantry. Barely pausing, Lowry chased Pancho Villa across Mexico at General Pershing's side, fought the Germans in France, and made a series of successful investments during the Florida Boom. In between, he saved a prisoner who was about to be hanged by facing down an angry Tampa mob. During WWII, he commanded the 56th Artillery Brigade, 31st Division in New Guinea. He returned to Tampa after the war to serve as Lieutenant General in the Florida National Guard.[13]

Millard Caldwell faced a Hobson's choice. He disapproved and disavowed President Truman's racial policies and liberal vision of America, but he also dismissed Governor Thurmond's Dixiecrat Party as ruinous to his beloved Democratic Party. A Yellow Dog Democrat, he was no barnburner and could not and would not fathom voting for a Republican. The campaign cleaved Florida into divisive camps and factions: conservative North Florida against an increasingly diverse and more moderate South Florida. Governor Caldwell encouraged fellow Florida Democrats to attend the States' Rights Convention while persuading them not to bolt the Democratic Party.[14]

The Democratic and Dixiecrat national conventions both met in early July 1948. "A Florida delegation divided on everything but opposition to a new term for President Truman," assembled in Philadelphia. In the past, state delegates traditionally composed "one big railroad party for the trip," but the split within the ranks made even a road trip impossible.[15]

The schism divided the party faithful across several issues and personalities, but also united strange bedfellows. Senator Pepper and Governor Caldwell still hoped that General Dwight David Eisenhower would be drafted at the convention as the party standard bearer. The Florida delegation was eager to endorse the revered hero of World War II. As late as the Fourth of July, Eisenhower hinted that he would accept the Democratic nomination—"if it is an honest draft." Dixiecrat-leaning delegates vowed to bolt the convention if President Truman was nominated. Pepper, according to an Associated Press reporter, "had been veering away from the President for months but had not come out nearly so flatly before." But on the eve of the convention, Eisenhower said "No," deflating the hopes of many. Pepper mounted a brief but ill-fated effort to secure the party nomination for himself. The *New York Times* characterized Pepper's move as "desperate." Ironically, few Florida delegates except Pepper swore allegiance to President Truman. Perhaps no Floridian worked harder to deny President Truman the nomination, and then made countless speeches to reelect the president. Truman, however, never forgave Pepper.[16]

The forty-eight-year-old Pepper, the South's most liberal senator, paid dearly for his missteps and miscalculations. Once considered unbeatable, a darling of President Roosevelt, Pepper now drew fire from a legion of enemies and former supporters. State newspapers blasted Pepper's behavior. The *St. Petersburg Times* was befuddled by Senator Pepper's behavior. "Almost three years ago," the paper editorialized in the wake of the political conventions, "we said—and emphatically—that we were against Claude Pepper for President. We still are—and even more so." The *Times* quoted a Texas editorial on the subject: "Today, we think we have witnessed Claude Pepper commit political hara-kiri." By 1948, an anti-Pepper faction had coalesced. St. Augustinians Charles E. Sheppard and Frank D. Upchurch enjoyed close ties with powerful men who dearly wanted Pepper defeated: Ed Ball, head of the duPont interests, and John Holliday Perry, a prominent newspaper publisher in the Southeast.[17]

Attorney General Watson added color to the political pandemonium of 1948, registering as an independent, and announcing his candidacy for governor. A native of Virginia, Watson began practicing law in Tampa in 1911. By 1915, he had become a municipal judge. Elected to the Florida legislature in 1930, he finished last in his race for governor in 1932. He later became an unsuccessful candidate for the State Supreme Court in 1938. Floridians elected the fiery Watson attorney general in 1940. A reporter called Watson "the scrappingest figure in Florida politics." Reelected in 1944, the irascible attorney general became a thorn in Governor Caldwell's side, as well as his fellow cabinet members and state unions. Watson angered Democrats by urging Dixiecrats to organize in Florida.[18]

The Dixiecrats concentrated their energies upon the Deep South states. In September, the Strom Thurmond caravan came to Florida. In Wildwood—the "crossroads of Florida"—Thurmond blasted lockstep "party loyalty," arguing that "States Rights programs" would have saved Germany from Hitler's masterplan.[19]

Predictably, the Democratic Convention was a three-ring circus. The civil rights plank in the party platform ignited protests, prompting a walkout by many Southern delegates. "This might be Charleston, South Carolina, in 1860," contemplated Senator Pepper. The entire Mississippi and half of the Alabama delegations left the building in protest of the civil rights plank. The Florida delegation remained. Charles E. Sheppard, a state legislator from St. Augustine, defended the insurgency. "We do not propose to tolerate any further interference in states' rights in the South."

On July 15, Dixiecrat nominee Thurmond told a boisterous crowd in Birmingham, "There's not enough troops in the army to force the southern people to break down segregation and admit the Negro race into our theaters, swimming pools, into schools, and into our homes." The next day in Charleston, Federal Judge J. Waties Waring, angry at the South Carolina Democratic Party's refusal to abide by the *Elmore v. Rice* ruling upholding the U.S. Supreme Court's decision on the white primary, ordered the Democratic Party to open its membership rolls to all.[20]

President Truman's nomination resembled a cross between a Pyrrhic victory and consolation prize. Florida cast nineteen and one-half votes for Senator Richard Russell of Georgia and one-half vote for an obscure federal administrator. Governor Caldwell and Senators Holland and Pepper cast their votes for Russell but maintained their loyalty to the Democratic Party. Few pundits expressed confidence that Truman would emerge victorious in November. Henrietta and Nelson Poynter, the publishers of the *St. Petersburg Times,* wrote from Philadelphia, "Southern delegates to the Democratic Convention came to the full realization last night that their side lost the Civil War in 1865. Some were angry—and they didn't know exactly where to turn. Some . . . walked out of the convention. Some of them threw away their votes—and many sulked." A fatigued and exasperated Claude Pepper admitted simply, "We're witnessing the complete breakup of the Democratic Party."[21]

The Progressive Party also held its convention in Philadelphia that fateful July. The party's standard bearer, Henry Wallace, had taken a beating on the stump and in the press. Kansas Congressman Herbert Meyer branded Wallace as "the evil tool of those who would destroy America." He asked, "When will the attorney general do his duty and indict this renegade?"[22]

When charges were hurled that the Progressive Party and Florida universities harbored communists, Governor Caldwell oddly defended academic freedom. Somewhat curiously, he saw no reason why a communist could not teach at a state university, providing the professor had been truthful. "I don't like boring from within," the governor told a gathering of law professors. "Complete academic freedom must be allowed if we are to grow," he argued. The editorial writer for the *Lakeland Ledger* translated the governor's message: "Our guess is that what he said was simply his uniquely left-handed way of saying that if there are in our institutions of higher learning Communists posing as patriotic Americans, let's get 'em out in a hurry." Caldwell, however, soon unleashed a clear and steady drumbeat of anti-communism. When accused of reckless red-baiting, Caldwell pointed out that President Truman signed Executive Order 9835, the so-called 1947 Loyalty Order, designed to identify and expel disloyal federal employees.[23]

If presidential elections were a horse race, September and October represent the stretch run. In 1948, commentators thought the election more closely resembled a four-ringed circus, complete with high-wire drama, rollicking crowds, and sadistic clowns. The election was as exciting as it was chaotic and confusing. In the campaign's final weeks, party officials implored Democrats to keep the faith and vote for Truman. The president excoriated Republicans on the stump, flailing the "Do Nothing Congress." Dixiecrats insisted Truman would lose Florida and the Deep South. Republicans exuded confidence; an optimism reinforced by every George Gallup poll that Thomas Dewey would usher in a new era of GOP rule. Dewey's decision not to campaign in the South dampened the enthusiasm. Progressive Party faithful believed in their cause and their candidate, even as the Cold War turned hotter and anti-communism became more hysterical.

Alarmingly, Dixiecrat supporters in Florida realized that neither the States' Rights Party nor its fire-eating candidate, Strom Thurmond, was on the ballot. Florida's election laws, fearful of challenges to the dominant Democracy, frowned upon third parties. When it was apparent that four Democratic Party electors were determined to cast their votes for Thurmond, legislators and party officials scrambled to assure that the Democratic Party triumphed in November while assuaging angry Dixiecrats and ignoring Henry Wallace supporters.

Questions swirled around the November ballot and Florida's quirky election law. That law required new parties, to qualify a place on the ballot, to persuade 5 percent of registered voters to change party affiliations and register with the new party prior to the primary. Democrats had already chosen delegates to the convention in the May primary. Florida election law stipulated that the ballots list only the names of the presidential electors of the respective parties, *not* the names of the presidential candidates. Frank D. Upchurch, a former mayor of St. Augustine and the chair of the Democratic Party's state delegation, also held the position of treasurer of the States' Rights Party. Upchurch, a state senator in 1943, had run unsuccessfully for governor in 1944 against Caldwell. His fellow St. Johns County neighbor, Charles E. Sheppard, was chairman of Florida's Dixiecrat Party. They were joined by Attorney General Watson, who also supported Strom Thurmond, and worked to recruit likeminded Democrats to undermine Truman. "Under pressure from the States' Rights forces," writes historian Kari Frederickson, "the state legislature overwhelmingly approved a change in the election law that would allow Truman, Dewey, and Thurmond—but not Progressive Party candidate Henry Wallace—on the ballot." Four Democratic electors had pledged their votes to Dixiecrat candidate Thurmond, not Democratic candidate Truman, which prompted the *Miami Herald* to sue to disqualify the electors who "violated their oath to the Democratic Party."[24]

Governor Caldwell settled the matter when he ordered the Florida Legislature to assemble for a rare September session. The *Lakeland Ledger* editorialized, "For this special session, Floridians can thank or blame President Truman and the undiscerning of the north who advised him to espouse the civil rights program at this critical moment in world history." A joint legislative committee attempted to clarify the muddled election laws. The committee agreed to placate the Dixiecrat States' Rights Party but resisted placing the Progressive Party on the ballot. Fewer than three thousand Floridians declared themselves Progressive Party members. Caldwell encouraged the legislature to pass a measure requiring the electors to vote for Truman if the president won Florida. He also encouraged that reluctant body to place Wallace and the Progressive Party ticket on the ballot. Without a place on the ballot for the party, the only way Wallace could win Florida's eight electoral votes would be to persuade voters to write in the names of eight Wallace electors. The governor urged legislators to be "eminently fair and allow a free and effective exercise of the right of franchise." Observed Allen Morris, "The man who wasn't there in the flesh—Henry Wallace—stood in spirit at the elbow of every member of the lame duck Florida legislature." The Florida Legislature, reported one paper, "with no liking for Henry Wallace or his politics, was about resigned tonight after a day of debate to accept him and put his name on the ballot." Morris observed that the "mildest" thing legislators could say about Wallace "was to describe him as the unconscious stooge of Stalin." Circuit Court Judge Miles W. Lewis ruled that the oaths were not legally binding. Electors had the right to vote their conscience. Ultimately, the Florida legislature was unable to legally exclude the Progressive Party ticket *and* include the Dixiecrat ticket on the Florida ballot.[25]

The Gordian knot had been cut, allowing Florida leaders to concentrate their energies on the state and local tickets. Caldwell urged voters to remain loyal to the party that had sheltered their fathers and grandfathers in stormy seas. In an October radio address, the governor praised Truman's "calm, courageous judgment," while lambasting the "do-nothing" 1946 Republican Congress. Gubernatorial candidate Fuller Warren, campaigning to succeed Caldwell, chose to ignore the national political races and emphasize state issues. Privately, Warren was convinced that Truman's campaign was doomed in Florida. In his travels around the state, Senator Pepper became convinced that the president would shock the experts and win the state and nation.[26]

Newspaper endorsements mattered in 1948. Truman's Little White House in Key West, a modest home that served as a winter retreat, helped secure the imprimatur of the *Key West Citizen*. The *Gainesville Sun* endorsed Strom Thurmond, as did many small newspapers in the Panhandle. The *Miami Herald*, South Florida's most influential newspaper, shocked the establishment when it endorsed Dewey. Meanwhile, the *Tampa Tribune's* managing editor Virgil "Red" Newton, despondent with the president, was convinced that Dewey was going to win the election. Yet he simply could not or would not support the Republican. The *Tribune,* for the first time in its history, declined to endorse any candidate. "We don't think that Truman has even an outside chance to be elected," editorialized the *St. Petersburg Times,* but the paper endorsed the "weak and unprepossessing" Democrat because he "has become a symbol to the rest of the world."[27]

On the eve of the election, the Ku Klux Klan paraded through several Lake County towns, harassing and threatening reporters. A series of cross burnings occurred in St. Petersburg and Fort Myers. One of the Kluxers told a reporter that they were committed to stopping "the communist movement in Florida." In Wildwood, fifty automobiles carrying Klansmen intimidated black voters, passing out letters warning, "Keep away from the polls."[28]

As nearly a half million Floridians filed to the polls on 2 November 1948, the betting line favored Dewey. The November first headline in the *St. Petersburg Evening Independent* announced, "Political Miracle Fails Truman; Dewey Is In." The *Tampa Tribune* headline, "DEWEY WINS," was printed and taken to the loading dock, only to be destroyed and substituted with the headline, "DEWEY, TRUMAN RUN CLOSE." *Tribune* editors or proofreaders, however, failed to change the headline of the lead editorial: "A Lame Duck President." The editorial asked, "Will President Truman invite President-elect Dewey to confer in meeting the immediate national and international problems?" Frank Upchurch predicted that Strom Thurmond would capture Florida and win the South.[29]

President Truman won the election of the century. Dixiecrats had weakened but not toppled the pillars of the Solid South, taking four states. Truman held Florida by a comfortable margin. The Dixiecrat Party's hopes were dashed, but Thurmond had run well in North Florida, securing at least 20 percent of the vote across the Panhandle and northern counties. Thurmond carried Alachua, Flagler, and St. Johns counties. Dewey secured one-third of Florida's vote, claiming five counties, and doubling Thurmond's vote.[30]

The Progressive Party registered barely a tremor in Florida, recording 11,620 votes. But what a tremor! Ybor City and West Tampa earned accolades and notoriety as Wallace country, where the progressive oracle somehow won seven of eleven precincts. It was the Progressive Party's most impressive political showing *outside* Manhattan. Ironically, in 1934, organized crime leaders in Ybor City and West Tampa had thwarted upstart Claude Pepper's bid to upset incumbent Senator Park Trammell. But in 1948, Wallace was victorious in those same Latin enclaves. To put the '48 election in perspective, in thirty-five Florida counties, Wallace received ten votes or fewer, but in Tampa he commanded 40 percent of his state total:

Harry Truman	291,988
Thomas Dewey	194,780
Strom Thurmond	89,750
Henry Wallace	11,620[31]

Wallace may have lost the election, but several of his most ardent supporters lost their jobs. Three instructors who openly supported the Progressive Party at the University of Miami were fired by the university.[32]

One week after the 1948 election, leaders of Florida's Democratic Party helped smooth and soothe ruffled feathers and bruised feelings. In Arcadia, the DeSoto County Elks Club hosted a barbecue. There, Attorney General Watson, the humiliated, erstwhile Democrat and unsuccessful candidate for governor, confronted his old nemesis, Governor Caldwell. "I personally thank each one of the members of the cabinet," remarked Caldwell, adding, "Even Tom Watson, as tough as he may be. Tom has a heart as big as a cow and horns about as bad." Watson rose, stating, "I agree with you," and then walked across the floor to shake hands with the governor. "The crowd cheered." State Representative Jerry Collins of Sarasota confessed that it had been a week of miracles: "First, President Truman was elected . . . and now Governor Caldwell and Mr. Watson are shaking hands!"[33]

The consequences of the 1948 election reverberated for decades. A year earlier, Senator Claude Pepper visited the Old State Capitol, where he began his political career as a freshman legislator from Taylor County in 1929. As he spoke, he noticed a single Republican, State Representative Alex Akerman Jr. of Orange County. Pepper proposed a law that "there should be one and just one Republican" in that august body so future generations could gawk at the extinct species. Pepper may have profited from the Solid South, but he was no prophet. Nor was his future lockset as Florida's senior statesman.[34]

Race, the 1948 Election, and Beyond

Amid the tumult of 1948, few Floridians would have regarded the arrest and beating of four young, black men accused of rape as a momentous event. In retrospect, the notorious episode echoed long after the events. The four young African Americans worked picking oranges in Groveland, located in Lake County. Author Gilbert King describes the setting: "What is certain is that Sheriff Willis McCall, from his first day in office [1944], understood that citrus was the engine that drove Lake County's economy, and he focused nearly all his efforts on issues surrounding labor." McCall, who quickly earned a reputation as die-hard segregationist and sadist, arrested the "Groveland Four" for raping a seventeen-year-old white girl in the summer of 1949. One of the young black men was killed in a manhunt. McCall ordered police to torture the prisoners in their jail cells in Tavares in order to coerce confessions.[35]

The *Orlando Sentinel* ran a front-page editorial cartoon depicting four empty electric chairs. Three of the men accused were sentenced to death. Later, when two of the condemned men won a new trial, Sheriff McCall escorted the men to Tavares on a lonely road. There, he shot two of the manacled suspects, claiming they were trying to escape. One died and the other was gravely wounded. Harry T. Moore hounded McCall, writing letters and rallying support, while NAACP lawyer Thurgood Marshall stared down a determined Ku Klux Klan and Southern legal system while valiantly defending the "Groveland boys." Caldwell would not be moved.

A coroner's jury absolved McCall. Repercussions followed. On Christmas Day 1951, Moore and his wife, Harriette, were celebrating the holiday and their silver wedding anniversary when a bomb destroyed their home. No one has ever been arrested for the crime. Authors Ben Green and Gilbert King argue that the Ku Klux Klan assassinated the Moores. Six Klansmen were implicated, but officials never filed charges. The bombing was not an isolated event; rather, it was the twelfth such explosion in Florida in 1951.[36]

The most incendiary and irreconcilable issue of 1948 was race. In Florida, Thurmond found his greatest success in the state's Black Belt, the northern counties between the Apalachicola and Suwannee rivers that contained disproportionate numbers of African Americans. But Florida's Black Belt was receding, not gaining, in importance. While the issue continued to fester in Florida in the decades after 1948, race no longer rattled and rendered Florida politics as it did in other Deep South states. Senator Thurmond triumphed in Louisiana, Alabama, Mississippi, and South Carolina, the four southern states with the highest proportion of African Americans. Indeed, since the 1920s, the Sunshine State had begun to separate from its neighbors as the region's least southern state. For over a century, Florida stood foursquare with Alabama and Georgia on the issue of race, sharing pride over traditions of slavery, Civil War and Reconstruction, the Bourbon Restoration, Jim Crow, and white primaries. But the South was also defined for its attachment to the land, its poverty, its high birth rates, its lack of immigrants, its rural traditions and small towns, and its preponderance of native inhabitants. By the late 1940s, huge swaths of Florida maintained only tenuous connections to Southern sectionalism and identity. Increasingly, new residents settled in the fast-growing regions of South and Central Florida. Newcomers were chiefly Northern transplants who were most concerned, not with race relations, but taxes, education, and lifestyle. Of course, many such transplants adjusted comfortably to the customs of Jim Crow. Lured by the Florida dream, many new Floridians hoped to achieve dignity in old age, enjoy a fresh start and a second chance. By 1950, Floridians typically were older, more ethnic, and more urban than their southern neighbors. They also were less rooted than their southern counterparts.[37]

Florida's divining rod pointed to Miami and the state's largest cities. By 1950, Miami had established the South's first all-Negro Municipal Court, with a black attorney serving as the judge of the new court. In 1949, Rev. Curtis Thomas Washington was ordained as the first black priest in the history of modern Florida. And in 1950, the University of Miami football team played against another squad fielding African American players. In 1945, Miami's black ministers had organized a "swim-in," securing a black public bathing area: Virginia Beach. By 1950, Florida's largest cities had hired black policemen. Sixty NAACP chapters, buoyed by the war's organizing spirit, had spread across the state. Finally, African Americans in the state's cities could reasonably expect to register and vote in the Democratic primaries, a rarity in the Deep South.[38]

The Rise of the Grand Old Party in Florida

An augury, the 1948 election exposed deep fissures in Florida's Democratic Party. Alienated and angry, voters only needed a respectable Republican candidate to scapegoat their frustrations. In 1948, Dewey succeeded in winning Broward, Orange, Palm Beach, Pinellas, and Sarasota counties, along with one-third of the statewide vote.

In Pinellas County, the revolution had already begun. Republicans had swept the county in 1946. So promising was Pinellas County that Ohio U.S. Senator Robert Taft, "Mr. Republican," visited Tarpon Springs, Dunedin, Clearwater, and St. Petersburg to boost the GOP chances. For decades, Northern and Midwestern transplants had been moving into Florida, bringing their deep-seated political culture with them. To many, their identity was ingrained in the Republican Party. Their grandfathers and great-grandfathers had fought to preserve the Union, and they remembered Grand Army of the Republic parades and GAR lodges in Keokuk, Kalamazoo, and Kankakee. In 1952, and again in 1956, Republican standard bearer Dwight David Eisenhower carried Florida. Ike's victories, however, did not constitute a political realignment, but signaled a message that moderate Democrats could pull the GOP lever on Election Day. By 1954, the Republican Party boasted six state legislators.[39]

Florida's divining rod bent to an unlikely place: Collier County. A sprawling landmass in the state's southwest, a swath of land, water, and swamp larger than the state of Delaware, Collier County must have seemed like an afterthought to 1940s politicians campaigning for office. In 1940, census takers counted barely five thousand residents. But Collier's fifty miles of undeveloped beaches and its subtropical isolation had begun to attract wealthy northern vacationers and investors. Once a haven and heaven for outlaws, tuberculars, and fishermen, Collier County became a bellwether for the Republican Party. In 1944, the *Collier County News* conducted a postcard poll of the registered voters. Remarkably, nearly two-thirds of the voters participated in the poll, representing what one newspaper described as "the first political poll taken in southwest Florida." The results were sobering to Democratic leaders: Fully 96 percent of voters expressed displeasure with the national party's policies. The GOP beckoned.[40]

History redeemed Collier County's disenchanted Democrats and Florida's Dixiecrats. Repudiated and humiliated by voters, the Dixiecrats ultimately rebounded, gradually morphing and merging into the modern Republican Party's southern wing. In 1954, the GOP scored a dramatic victory when St. Petersburg Republican Bill Cramer won election to the U.S. Congress in the Tampa Bay area. Support came largely from transplanted Republicans, not embittered Dixiecrats. Cramer's election signified the first chink in the Democratic armor. No Southern Republican had been elected to Congress since Reconstruction. The decade of the 1960s witnessed greater Republican triumphs in Florida. White backlash—the result of angst over crime and integration, an unpopular war, and the Great Society—helped elect Florida's first modern Republican U.S. Senator (Edward J. Gurney) and first modern governor (Claude Kirk). The heartlands of the GOP shifted from the Midwest in the 1950s to the South in the 1980s. By the end of the century, white Southern Democrats had become an endangered species.[41]

The 1948 Governor's Race

Amidst the 1948 political cyclone, Floridians elected a new governor. The race proved to be memorable. Fuller Warren, an ambitious lawyer and bombastic orator from Blountstown faced off against J. Tom Watson, the dyspeptic attorney general, and Dan McCarty, a World War II hero, citrus grower, and legislator from Fort Pierce. Once a member of the Ku Klux Klan, McCarty now disavowed the organization. While privately backing McCarty, Caldwell vowed to stay out of the gubernatorial race, reminding journalists that he admired the "utter independence" of state voters. Warren charged that a "Caldwell combine" conspired against him, wishing to perpetuate itself through McCarty. The governor furiously denied the charges.[42]

The *Miami Herald* speculated that if the more politically conservative McCarty defeated Warren, the victory would signify a favorable climate for Caldwell to challenge Senator Claude Pepper in 1950. Caldwell not only disapproved of Warren's populist leanings and coarse behavior, he also personally disliked Warren's shady friends (gamblers) and had not forgotten Warren's duplicity at the 1948 Democratic convention. Caldwell prepared a statement criticizing Warren, but never released it. In a nasty run-off against McCarty, Warren prevailed, but in his hell-bent effort to finance his expensive campaign, he owed favors. The governor-elect accused the outgoing governor of leaving the state financial coffers empty with hefty bills to be paid. "The war surplus has been spent," a dejected Warren told the 1949 legislature. "The day of reckoning is at hand."[43]

As Governor Caldwell's term was closing, he announced his plans: "My intention is to practice law, live on my farm and enjoy the pleasures of private living." He reflected that the modernization of Florida's school system was his proudest accomplishment, while his efforts at conservation the least successful. He chuckled that an early effort to prod the University of Florida football team was his most controversial action. He pointed to a new coach and a more respectable Gator team in 1948 as vindication.[44]

Governor Caldwell would not miss answering the many letters that asked for favors. One such missive stands out. M. F. Whitaker, a farmer in Bristol, wrote: "Your Excellency: My hog has been stolen by a man here.... Please help me to get this crime prosecuted." Some letters, however, clearly brightened the governor's mood. The Honorable W. J. Sears Jr. wrote the governor, enclosing a book, *The Bobwhite Quail*. "I bought the book for you because I know you cannot shoot them . . ." explained Sears. He also queried whether Caldwell had encountered the species. "Fortunately," the governor responded, disabusing the letter writer of the image of the governor as a city dweller who gets queasy around the topic of hunting, "I do not have to restrict my acquaintance with the bird to academic research—I have practical knowledge not only of his standing and flying qualities but, also, the ways and means of taking him." He added, "P.S. I am going to Georgia this afternoon to kill a turkey." On another occasion, the governor was asked to become a member of the American Fox Hunters Association. Today, politicians would run away from this request, yelping like a hound dog. But Caldwell responded, "I will be glad to accept membership in this organization and would enjoy, if time permits, attending one of the hunts in this area." Caldwell even suggested the letter writer contact Florida's Game and Fresh Water Fish Commission, regarding "the matter of a bounty on fox."[45]

On 5 January 1949, Governor Caldwell turned over the reins of state government to newly elected Fuller Warren. "By mid-morning," *Time* magazine's correspondent reported, despite a drizzling rain, one of the biggest crowds in Tallahassee's history was standing in front of Florida's steepled old state capitol. . . . The rain forced dignified Governor Millard F. Caldwell to cut short his resumé of his administration. But it stopped as soon as the new man, handsome, greying, jovial Fuller Warren stepped up to the podium."[46]

The Inauguration of Fuller Warren, January 1949, Tallahassee. Governors Warren and Caldwell exchange pleasantries. Courtesy State Archives of Florida, Florida Memory. https://www.floridamemory.com/items/show/68775.

The reporter added, "The folks expected a good show. They got it." The new governor invoked his promise to eliminate "roaming livestock from the roads." Before the crowd dove into trays holding forty thousand pounds of barbecue, Governor Warren thanked Governor Caldwell, remarking, "He has been generous in letting bygones be bygones."[47]

Caldwell and Florida: The 1940s

The decade of the 1940s had taken the State of Florida on a wild roller coaster ride. In 1940, Caldwell was an unhappy U.S. congressman, on the eve of his return to his beloved Florida. In 1940, Arkansas and South Carolina both outranked Florida in population. But the war and its concentrated energies had catapulted Florida to new heights. The decade's growth arc was especially striking when compared to other Southern states. Florida gained nearly a million new residents between 1940 and 1950, *more* than the *combined* demographic gains of Alabama, Mississippi, Georgia, and South Carolina. In 1950, Florida's population of 2,771,305 surpassed Arkansas and South Carolina, but also moved ahead of Iowa, Connecticut, Kansas, Maryland, West Virginia, Mississippi, and Louisiana.[48]

Writing in *Fortune* magazine in 1948, Lawrence Lessing captured the postwar pulse when he described what was happening to America's southernmost state: "Florida enacts some essential melodrama of America, seen in a distorted mirror." Visitors to St. Petersburg or Miami Beach could observe firsthand the startling images. Florida, historically one of America's most youthful states, was acquiring touches of silver rinse and gray. By 1950, the median age of Miami Beach was forty-three, rising to fifty-four by the end of the decade. No American city had ever boasted such figures. Tourists detected a strange accent (Yiddish) as many of the newcomers were Eastern European Jewish immigrants. No Southern county rivaled Dade's demographics: Its population included more New Yorkers than Georgians, more Michiganders than Alabamians. In St. Petersburg, the demographic rarity had occurred earlier and evolved more slowly. By the 1920s, city fathers had created an industry catering to retirees: dozens of cafeterias, shuffleboard and horseshoe courts, boarding houses and seasonal apartments, and societies such as the Three-Quarter Century Club. By 1950, the census confirmed what every motorist and shuffleboard court manager already knew: almost one-quarter of the city's residents were sixty-five and older. Among white residents, the proportion was considerably higher.[49]

The source of Florida's dynamic growth resulted from sustained migrations, not from an internal baby boom or a single event or source. The history of modern Florida can be interpreted through the dizzying set of migrations involving individuals, families, and groups. Military veterans, New York Jews and Italians, Midwestern retirees, and Caribbean immigrants flocked to the Sunshine State in the 1940s and beyond. Florida was becoming a state of fresh starts and second chances. The decade intensified what had been distinctive features of America: restlessness and rootlessness. In 1947, fully seventy million Americans were no longer living in the same house in which they had resided in 1940. Florida was fast becoming a place where almost everyone came from someplace else. In 1930, slightly over half of Floridians were natives born in the state. By 1950, that percentage had fallen to 43.5 percent, plunging to 36 percent a decade later.[50]

Millard Caldwell adjusted uncomfortably to the profound changes sweeping across Florida. Caldwell's bedrock had always been his past and present ties to rural Florida. But since the 1920s, white and black Floridians had been fleeing rural hamlets and plantations for the urban North and cities such as Jacksonville, Orlando, and Miami. The decade of the Forties witnessed stagnation and decline in the Panhandle and North Florida, its timber largely cleared, its cotton no longer profitable, and its workforce unsettled or resettled. During the decade, the counties of Baker, Calhoun, Dixie, Flagler, Gilchrist, Hamilton, Holmes, Levy, Jackson, Jefferson, Liberty, Madison, Suwannee, Taylor, Wakulla, and Washington recorded a collective *loss* of 13,361 persons. During the same period, the counties of Dade, Duval, Hillsborough, Orange, and Pinellas *gained* one-half million newcomers. In 1900, two of every three Floridians lived in North Florida; by midcentury, only one in three resided in the region. Governors Millard Caldwell and Fuller Warren, hailing from Milton, Blountstown, and Tallahassee, were becoming anachronisms.[51]

Caldwell's hometown and backyard could not avoid change. The Capitol City, a modest town of only 16,000 inhabitants on the eve of Pearl Harbor, swelled to 27,237 residents by 1950. Attracted by wartime demands and governmental bureaucracies, black and white students, pink- and white-collar workers, rural transplants, and students flocked to Tallahassee. Leon County's population grew by more than 60 percent, from around thirty thousand residents to over fifty-one thousand by 1950.[52]

4

CITIZEN, COLD WARRIOR, CIVIL DEFENSE DIRECTOR, AND JUDGE

1950–1970

On the eve of 1950, the press concurred that Caldwell would run against his old foe and Tallahassee neighbor, Senator Claude Pepper. The *Tampa Tribune* fantasized, "What a grand campaign it would be with a man like Caldwell and Pepper slugging it out!" Caldwell would have almost certainly defeated Pepper in the 1950 U.S. Senate race. However, during a June 1949 visit to Washington, DC, he told friends and journalists that he was "not even remotely interested" in challenging Pepper. Caldwell, however, paid a special visit to Congressman George A. Smathers, who occupied the same office Congressman Caldwell once claimed.[1]

Millard Caldwell told friends he would never run for political office again. His family loved their Harwood estate. For decades, however, rumors circulated that he was prepared to run, once again, for governor. Instead, he accepted several high-level positions. Why did he not run and almost certainly defeat Claude Pepper in the race for U.S. Senate? The short answer is that he hated Washington. The long answer leads with the question of why he rejected the U.S. Senate for an administrative job in Washington? The only rational explanation is that Caldwell believed in public service, and when the president asks you to serve, you answer the call.[2]

In 1950, as Cold War tensions turned hot in Korea and atomic blasts radiated from Kazakhstan, President Truman created the Federal Civil Defense Administration by executive order, followed by Congressional enactment of the Federal Civil Defense Act (FCDA). As McCarthyism peppered public debates and popular culture, President Truman appointed Caldwell as the first head of the U.S. Civilian Defense Administration. Truman wanted a leader who had governed at the national and state levels. A chastened Caldwell later told friends that he only accepted the position after persuasion over bourbon with Potomac River water and a game of poker with Congressman Sam Rayburn and U.S. Senator Lyndon B. Johnson. Caldwell had served in the U.S. Congress with both men, and he and Rayburn were native Tennesseans. Caldwell headed a vast bureaucracy of civilian defense activities designed to protect Americans from an enemy attack. The new director embodied postwar American attitudes, bringing credentials as a cold warrior and a radioactive anti-communist.[3]

President Truman, not wishing to be branded soft on communism, issued Executive Order 9835 in March 1947. The draconian order required loyalty oaths of public employees. As governor of Florida, Caldwell urged local and state authorities to purge communists from the ranks of schoolteachers, professors, and staff. In 1948, Governor Caldwell and legislators had incorporated the loyalty oaths into law. All state employees, from the governor to state employees and elected officials, were required to take the oath, beginning: "I . . . solemnly swear that I will support the Constitution of the United States and of the State of Florida; that I am not a member of the Communist Party . . . that I do not believe in the overthrow of the Government of the United States or the State of Florida by violence." Patriotic organizations, such as the American Legion, participated in the "Anti-Red" expulsions. In 1951, Jacksonville's City Council passed a law forbidding members of the Communist Party from residing within the city limits.[4]

Addressing college students in 1951, Caldwell reflected upon what historians later called the "Munich analogy," the failure of contemporaries

Millard Caldwell, Director of the Federal Civil Defense Administration, Washington, DC. Courtesy State Archives of Florida, Florida Memory. https://www.floridamemory.com/items/show/133598.

to confront Hitler when he threatened Czechoslovakia in 1938. Instead, British and French leaders appeased the dictator, resulting in cataclysmic consequences. Caldwell, praised by the *St. Petersburg Times* for his clarity and prose, argued that America had blundered after the end of World War II by not realizing that the ultimate freedom was "freedom of knowledge." He continued, "We hadn't thought that so long as nations of men oppose liberty, freedom means a readiness to pay whatever price the strength of the opposition entails. The only choice we had, though few realized the fact, was whether to accept hardship then, or later. We chose—later. It is later now."[5]

Implementing his principles, Director Caldwell advanced a two-prong approach, insisting that America must contain communism abroad while home-front Americans prepared for nuclear war. Under Caldwell's leadership, Alert America inculcated the doctrine of preparedness. "Civil defense . . . begins at home." Fortress America, promised the new director, served as a "national insurance policy." Alert America sent a civil defense exhibit across the country, an effort Caldwell dubbed "Paul Revere on Wheels." As the head of an agency to protect the home front, he asked Congress for $300 million for state matching funds to construct bomb shelters, as part of the so-called "Caldwell Shelter Program." Fallout shelters followed. Arguing that all Americans were imperiled by Soviet aggression, Caldwell hoped civil defense might unite the country.[6]

Caldwell's disdain for Washington only intensified when Congress rejected all funding for shelters in 1951, 1952, and 1953. The requests failed for several reasons. Congress was never convinced that civil defense was a federal matter. "The most vicious enemy in America," admitted Caldwell, "was the shocking apathy of the American people to their danger from enemy attack." Moreover, the sales tag was enormous. For example, officials in New York City discovered that supplying individual identification tags for all the boroughs' schoolchildren would require 62,500 pounds of nickel silver, not even considering the public relations and emotional costs. Residents of Florida's cities soon conducted air raid drills while children learned the meaning of duck and cover. Civil defense had become a moral and patriotic duty. Caldwell and the new agency, argues a historian, "intended shelters serving as the centerpiece of America's civil defense effort."[7]

Neither Congress nor Stalin proved to be Caldwell's most nagging problem; rather, it was reconciling how his fundamental beliefs in racial segregation and civic equality squared with his pleas for shared sacrifice.

Race, ethnicity, and privilege (propaganda posters promised) stopped at the bomb shelter door. An angry President Truman should not have been shocked that Caldwell defined the Red menace in black and white. Martin Friedman, a special assistant to the president, recalled Caldwell's interview with Truman. The Floridian candidly warned President Truman: "I just wanted you to know my outlook on civil rights and yours are not the same and I can't change my outlook." President Truman's announcement of Caldwell's appointment galvanized opposition. Civil rights groups, acutely aware of the governor's record on race, attempted to block his appointment. The NAACP, writes historian Laura McEnaney, "insisted that his support of segregation during his political career in Florida made him unfit to head a federal agency that was supposed to protect *all* citizens from nuclear danger." Florida's NAACP leader Harry T. Moore and Walter White, the organization's executive director, both testified against Caldwell. *Crisis,* the magazine of the NAACP, informed readers in March 1951 that "The Florida state conference of branches has registered a strong protest against the appointment of ex-governor Millard Caldwell as administrator of civil defense." U.S. Senator Lyndon Johnson received letters from Texas NAACP chapters urging him to vote against the nominee Johnson helped select for the position. "I shall keep your view in mind," Johnson politely replied to protesters.[8]

Other critics accused Caldwell of racism when he encouraged locales to build and implement segregated bomb shelters. Perhaps most damaging, Caldwell infuriated African American leaders when he refused to address them respectfully by their surname or title. "I reserve the right to address any such person . . . in such manner as I please, and in accordance with my own views," Caldwell countered, projecting a southern patrician demeanor. President Truman was highly embarrassed by the passionate attacks, but he nonetheless supported his nominee, who received Congressional confirmation. U.S. Senator Lyndon Johnson and Texas Congressman Sam Rayburn provided the embattled nominee cover.[9]

Millard Caldwell's tenure as America's first civil defense administrator can, at best, be described as something between a debacle and an embarrassment. His return to the national stage revealed that the former congressman and governor was tone deaf in a world changing around him. He would soon judge the pace and legality of change. He was not alone.

Some historians have suggested that the decade of the 1950s ended in Dallas, Texas, in November 1963. The Lyndon B. Johnson that cajoled and cudgeled colleagues to vote for Millard Caldwell's appointment in 1951 became president in 1963. Johnson, by sheer force and propitious timing, conceived and delivered the Great Society and its landmark laws: Voting Rights Acts, etc. While Johnson had shifted his views on race and government, Caldwell had stood his ground. In Florida, Caldwell was joined by many residents who detested the social changes sweeping the nation and the Sunshine State. None found the changes as abominable as Ed Ball.

Mister Ball

More than any other Floridian, Ed Ball appreciated Viscount Palmerston's famous reply to a member of Parliament: "Sir, Great Britain has no friends, only interests." Flinty, irascible, and parsimonious, Ed Ball wielded more power than anyone in the state's history. He never held political office but was one of the most investigated and litigated figures in state history. On several occasions, Caldwell, under oath, testified in defense of Ball. On one occasion, he described Ball as a model of simplicity, a man so unpretentious that he did not own an automobile, even though he was General Motor's largest shareholder. "It wasn't so much that he was tight," remembered Raymond Mason, a longtime confidante and biographer of Ball. "He had no desire for material things." When filling out applications that asked his profession, Ball put down "agriculture"—because he tended to pine trees.[10]

Jake Belin, a longtime associate and executor of the Ball estate, wished biographers luck in documenting Mr. Ball's actions. "He did not want to preserve any correspondence," Belin recalled. "His idea was: 'Do not say too much, for you will get your foot in your mouth, and you are just making a living for lawyers if you do.'" The courtly Ball neither smoked nor sat when a woman entered the room. His assistant painted his manners and morals: "He [Ball] was a very private man. He never took off his coat. He did not want anybody to come to the office without a coat. He dressed formally . . . He was immaculate . . . He could not stand vulgarisms." Ball also expected his associates to labor as hard as he did, which meant working on weekends and holidays. "They did not mean a thing to him," sighed Belin. Wherever he traveled, Ball insisted on keeping his watch set on Jacksonville time. Belin worked tirelessly for and with the irascible tyrant for more than a half century, respectfully calling his mentor and boss, "Mr. Ball."[11]

Caldwell and Ball shared a deep affection for the Old South and its culture. Whereas Caldwell was to the plantation born, an affable host and raconteur, Ball lacked the former's birthright, charm, education, and wit. Caldwell was tall and handsome whereas Ball was short and balding. But Ball possessed a determined focus and ferocity that his friend lacked. They both embraced conservative government, although they differed when it came to the question of whom should shoulder the burden of taxes. Caldwell displayed a populist streak that alarmed Ball.

The son of a Confederate cavalry captain, Ed Ball was born in Hopewell, Virginia, in 1888. He abhorred the evil twins of racial integration and progressivism. He dropped out of school at age thirteen to guard his father's oyster beds from thieves. He worked as a hardware store clerk in California and prospected for gold in the Klondike. His fortunes literally and figuratively pivoted upon his sister's marriage to one of the wealthiest men in America. In 1921, thirty-seven-year-old Jessie Dew Ball married fifty-seven-year-old Alfred Irénée duPont. Ed Ball soon began managing some of his brother-in-law's sprawling business interests. Rejecting the glitter of Florida's Gold Coast during the Land Boom, duPont and Ball invested heavily in North Florida. "Mr. Ball said he wanted to buy land to plant pine trees," recalled a lifetime associate and confidante, B. K. Roberts. "They [local Crackers] had never heard of such a thing. 'That crazy Yankee will soon go broke,' they used to say."[12]

When South Florida real estate cratered in 1926, Alfred duPont realized his brother-in-law was shrewd and farsighted. While Ball had no experience in the banking business, he understood that reputation and solvency were paramount. The duPont-Ball team invested heavily in the First National Bank. When First National survived Florida's crash, they won the confidence of businessmen. Later, First National's cards reminded patrons: "NO EDWARD BALL-OWNED BANK EVER FAILED." When duPont died in 1935, Ed became a trustee of the estate, and he proceeded to buy banks, railroads, a telephone company, paper mills, newspapers, depressed farmsteads, and cut-over forests. Mr. Ball liked to connect the dots. Intrigued with the rush of automobiles crowding Florida, he proceeded to buy corner lots in the state's major cities. Once purchased, he tore down any built structures to reduce taxes. Ball had pioneered a new enterprise: the parking lot. DuPont's estate was valued at $33 million at his death. When Ed Ball died in 1981, the estate had grown to $2 billion. As the chief trustee of the duPont holdings, he had become the state's largest landowner, as well as the biggest banker and railroader.[13]

Upon hearing the news of statehood in 1845, the *East Florida Whig News* dolefully warned, "The day of the trial has come, people will soon feel the benefits of the tax collector." Ed Ball, too, realized that the Florida Legislature could be a businessman's worst and best friend. He ensured that his empire remained intact through strategic investments in political favors and retribution. He was often called "the power" behind Florida's fabled "Pork Chop Gang." Pork Choppers befriended Ball's properties, making Florida one of America's great tax shelters. Floridians or their corporations, explained Gene M. Burnett, paid "no income tax, no state property tax, no corporate income tax, and no severance tax on natural resources." Friends in the Legislature ensured that Ball's company towns in the sparsely settled Panhandle, such as Port St. Joe, enjoyed exceptionally well-paved, modern highways.[14]

To entertain politicians, he purchased four thousand acres in 1934 and three years later built the rustic Wakulla Lodge on the picturesque Wakulla

River. Decades later, when an environmental group disagreed with his policies, he simply installed a fence across the river, keeping out boaters and birders. Reacting to critics, friends of Ball retorted, "Edward Ball promoted no massive developments, no land-consuming golf courses . . ." The Wakulla Lodge became a favorite retreat for legislators anxious to escape the prying press and conduct business. He famously gathered his associates at the end of a long business day, raising his glass of Old Forester bourbon to the toast, "Confusion to the enemy!"[15]

"People at the St. Joe company," insisted Diane Roberts, "would tell you that Ed Ball got up every morning and asked, 'Who do we fight today?' If there was a clear answer, he'd call B. K. Roberts, who was happy to take care of problems from women to governors to corporations." Ball carved out a reputation as a no-holds-barred financier who understood the art of the deal. He also understood the power of friends in high places. His divorce lawyer, B. K. Roberts, a distant cousin of Professor Diane Roberts, became Chief Justice of the Florida Supreme Court, alongside former governor Millard Caldwell. Ball's nemeses occasionally matched their rival in stature. Ball crossed swords with Governor LeRoy Collins on many occasions. "He was always trying to accomplish some private interest of his own," remembered Collins, adding, "He was difficult to get together with because he liked to have his own way."[16]

For someone who was extraordinarily successful in avoiding paying taxes, Ball spent decades and considerable resources persuading Florida legislators *to impose* a state sales tax. Ball knew that a dynamic, growing Florida desperately needed increasing revenues to pay for state services. Since taxing corporations represented a progressive and popular option, Ball lobbied for a state sales tax, which, of course was regressive and unpopular with voters. Most importantly, a sales tax discouraged taxing the wealthy. Ball marshaled considerable political capital to achieve his goals.[17]

"The nearest thing to a statewide political boss," argued journalist Martin Dyckman, "was not a politician in the conventional sense." Ed Ball fulfilled that role. When asked about Ball's clout, Jake Belin explained: "Ball did not make political contributions. He had power over people. He had influence over votes; he delivered votes. . . . If you are in control of one of the largest banking institutions in the state, you are going to have muscles." Illustrative of Ball's clout, LeRoy Collins aspired to become Speaker of the Florida House of Representatives for the 1939 session. His rival was G. Pierce Wood, who just happened to be a Liberty County forester who supplied pulpwood to the St. Joe Paper Company. Collins, who supported a progressive sales tax to balance the state budget, lost to Wood. The *Tampa Tribune* headline underscored the melding of politics and business: "House Picks DuPont Man."[18]

While Ball enthusiastically supported Caldwell's candidacy for governor in 1944, Caldwell demonstrated his independence by opposing a state sales tax. "Millard was just like Ball," explained Jake Belin, who knew both men intimately. "He [Caldwell] was a fighter. And they fought." Ball won this battle. In 1948, Ball supported Fuller Warren for governorship, while Caldwell favored Dan McCarty. Warren became the last rural, small-town Floridian elected governor. Although pledging to veto any sales tax, economic conditions deteriorated so severely that Warren reluctantly signed the measure in a special session, saying famously, "I'll go along with it, but don't call it a sales tax." Warren finessed it as a gross receipts tax. "Same damn thing," deadpanned Belin. Special interests ensured that the tax did not apply to rent, food, medicine, and a host of other items. Merchants placed jars on counters with labeling reading, "Pennies for Fuller." Ball and friends extracted a measure of revenge by helping identify myriad exemptions to the three cents tax. "Justice B. K. Roberts," observed Diane Roberts, "helped draft the sales tax bill in his own study." She added, "The judge might one day have to rule on its constitutionality, but surely he could still be perfectly impartial." Warren had appointed Roberts chief justice just days earlier. As a young law student in the 1950s, Buddy Mackay reminisced how he "stumbled on the master index of political power in Florida"—the state's tax code. "Those people with political power, like businesses, lawyers, doctors, architects . . . and anyone remotely connected to agriculture, had simply seen to it that the products and services sold by them were exempt from the sales tax."[19]

Ball's most dangerous, dedicated, and intelligent adversary was U.S. Senator Claude Pepper. Pepper charged that Ball had created a duPont monopoly and should not be permitted to operate the Florida East Coast Railway. "The sinister and dangerous character of Ball's domination of the State of Florida becomes more distinct as one sees it more clearly," Pepper wrote in his diary on 23 January 1946. It would not be Pepper's last rant against his adversary.[20]

Red Pepper vs. George Smathers: 1950

If Millard Caldwell returned to Washington riding a wave of anti-communism and a turbo-charged Cold War, Claude Pepper exited the Capitol for the same reasons. For decades, Pepper seemed invulnerable. First appointed and then elected to the U.S. Senate in the 1930s, Pepper was all things to all Floridians: a hawk on defense and military appropriations; a fist-thumping populist, reminding Floridians of his support for Social Security and opposition to the Poll Tax; and a Southerner, reminding voters of his Alabama roots and Confederate ancestors, voting *against* a national lynching law, and loudly criticizing his opposition to the U.S. Supreme Court's decision to outlaw the white primary. Claude Pepper and Millard Caldwell voted against every Congressional effort to make lynching a national crime. In January 1938, a young, ambitious Florida lawyer, Fuller Warren, wrote Pepper, noting that he had read the Senator's speech against the anti-lynching bill. "I think it is the ablest speech that you have ever made," Warren gushed. It was Claude Pepper, not Caldwell or Warren, who, when the press asked his opinion of *Smith v. Allwright* (1944), demagogued: "Southerners will not allow matters peculiar to us to be determined by those who do not know our problems." In his private diary, Pepper was more introspective and honest, writing, "The Negro question is a difficult and tragic one." Even the most ardent Southern liberal had to trim his sails on the race question.[21]

Millard Caldwell and Claude Pepper may have been Democrats and fellow residents of small-town Tallahassee, but they genuinely disliked one another. Whereas Caldwell was a patrician who inherited a fortune along with fortunate good looks, Pepper grew up in a small Alabama town and suffered from a terrible case of acne. Caldwell was a gifted collegiate athlete while Pepper endured poverty and shoveled coal to attend the University of Alabama. Both men volunteered for service in the Great War. Caldwell lived on a plantation home in Leon County, while his rival moved from Homosassa to Perry to Tallahassee. Staunch Democrats, Pepper idolized Franklin Roosevelt and the New Deal, whereas Caldwell expressed distaste for FDR's policies and consequences. Pepper grasped power to expand the role of government while Caldwell believed in the Jeffersonian ideal that the best government was the least government.

Pepper was a rarity in Washington: a Southern liberal. He was a darling of labor unions and construction companies, entities that thrived during the war years. Whereas Ball and Caldwell loathed President Roosevelt, comparing the New Deal to Soviet collectivism, Pepper idolized the chief executive. When *Time* magazine featured Pepper on its 2 May 1938 cover, the title page introduced Americans to "Roosevelt's weather cock." Throughout the 1930s and '40s, he attracted a number of enemies who hoped to abort his political career. By 1944, the list was growing: Ed Ball, Associated Industries, Millard Caldwell, and Southern conservatives.[22]

The harbinger of Pepper's demise—some scholars would argue self-destruction—occurred in 1944. Pepper was running for reelection in what seemed a cakewalk. After all, President Roosevelt was running for a fourth term, the economy was booming, and the Allies were winning the war. Moreover, Democratic opponents were lackluster. Then, two months before the May primary, Judge J. Ollie Edmunds threw his hat into the ring. Born into poverty, Edmunds's story was part Horatio Alger, part Claude Pepper. Through luck and pluck, he graduated from high school and Stetson University. In 1934 Judge Edmunds supported Pepper in his first race for the U.S. Senate. An inexperienced politician, Edmunds received $60,000 from Ball and an associate to boost his campaign. Pepper admitted in his diary that "the opposition [is] bitter and determined." Pepper won the Democratic primary; however, if his foes were looking for an omen, the candidate won only 51.4 percent of the vote against a weak field.[23]

Between 1944 and Pepper's reelection in 1950, the political climate had become polarized. When the war ended in September 1945, the United States, like Caesar's Rome, "bestrode the world like a colossus." But another superpower had emerged from the chaos of war: the Soviet Union.

Somehow blindsided by his seeming invincibility, Pepper committed too many missteps. A glimpse at Pepper's diary entries in January 1946 is revealing. "To Miami Beach and addressed 794 who paid $2.00 per plate under the auspices of the Soviet American Committee and a splendid meeting. My speech on Russia." Not only had Pepper visited the Soviet Union, but he told the American people that Uncle Joe could be "trusted" and asked that we "pray for his health." Three days later, the senator met with James M. Cox, a former Ohio governor who ran as a Democratic candidate for president in 1920. In 1923 Cox purchased the newspaper that evolved into the *Miami Daily News.* Cox advised Pepper "to take liberal leadership in the country—not to bother too much about local politics in Florida." On 11 January, Pepper summarized "a frank talk to mostly reactionaries" in Tallahassee. The following day he entertained "a delegation of doctors" at his Washington home. "I told [them] I was going to support a compulsory prepayment plan of medical and hospital care." On 15 January, he reflected, "Jacksonville is the most reactionary city in the state. All they want to do is betray the people." Pepper never realized or wanted to understand the reasons why Floridians were losing faith in his leadership. Overweening of his righteous causes, Pepper wore blinders while providing his enemies ample ammunition.[24]

In May 1946, Senator Pepper's diary entry read, "President Truman has lost the liberal and labor vote and doomed his party and maybe himself." Pepper's political future, too, was increasingly fraught with doubt. He was only forty-six years old. Smathers's biographer Brian Lewis Crispell argues, "Claude Pepper's instinctive liberalism, combined with encouragement from intellectuals like Raymond Robbins, help explain his increasingly controversial stands favoring Stalinist Russia as well as his general suspicions of business interests."[25]

How ironic that following the hurly burly of 1948 that it would be Claude Pepper, not Strom Thurmond, who faced political danger. Political insiders were still betting that Pepper's worst nightmare was Caldwell. In late July 1949, J. D. Bodman wrote Caldwell, insisting that "Pepper is a menace to the American system of government, that he is a socialist, almost a Communist." A few days later, Caldwell received a single-spaced one-page letter from James Ball Jr., a prominent businessman in Belle Glade. He urged his old friend to run against Pepper. "Millard, if you decide to run let me know so that I can start the propaganda at an early date. I want to be in your corner from the beginning." Caldwell replied in his typically honest manner: "Jimmy, Thank you for your note. I can arouse no enthusiasm in that thing." The last comment may be the most eloquent explanation as to why Caldwell declined a sure seat in the U.S. Senate.[26]

In 1950, Pepper's enemies carefully and desperately searched for an opponent possessing charisma and kryptonite. In the spring of 1949, Pepper wrote his old friend Raymond Robins—who had witnessed firsthand the Bolshevik Revolution in Russia—that he suspected Millard Caldwell or George Smathers would oppose him. Caldwell deferred to the youngblood congressman.[27]

George Smathers was "the natural." The thirty-six-year-old Miami congressman had led a charmed life. An outstanding athlete at Miami Senior High School, he was offered a football scholarship to the University of Illinois, Red Grange's alma mater. Judge Frank Smathers recognized his son's off-the-field skills and steered him to the University of Florida, where he could cultivate lifelong political and social connections. Tall, handsome, and athletic, George was a cheerleader, captain of the basketball team, and president of the student body at the University of Florida. Ironically, the young collegian first met Pepper in 1938 when the senator was running for reelection. Smathers recalled the meeting, "He [Pepper] asked me, would I manage his campaign on the campus for reelection? I was so flattered that I immediately accepted that kind of invitation." Smathers was also a war hero, a square-jawed Marine who had pestered local recruiters to become a fighting leatherneck. He managed to escape a desk job for combat in the South Pacific. He befriended backers willing to raise lots of money to defeat Pepper. President Truman, who never forgave Pepper for his slight in 1948, summoned the little-known congressman to the White House with a simple command: "I want you to beat that son-of-a-bitch Claude Pepper!" Pitch perfect, Smathers's politics and profile aligned with the public mood.[28]

Once a master of mullet fish fry oratory and darling of the editorial boards, Pepper failed miserably convincing the state's leading newspapers that he deserved another term in Washington. Pepper had always commanded respect from journalists, but among the state's leading dailies, only the *St. Petersburg Times* and *Daytona Beach News-Journal* endorsed the incumbent. Withering editorials undercut the once popular populist. The *Miami Herald* depicted the race "as a trial of radicalism and extremism," while the *Tampa Daily Times* accused Pepper of being a "Stalin apologist."[29]

The 1950 election entered the annals of political history as one of the dirtiest campaigns ever conducted. The election served as a vote of confidence for Wisconsin's U.S. Senator Joe McCarthy, the most revered and despised man in Washington. Many Americans first read about the Smathers-Pepper race in the 20 April 1950 issue of *Time* magazine. The popular periodical once again proved that history is not what happened but what people *think* happened. The fact that no one has ever verified Smathers's mythical one-liners has not dulled our appetite for gossip. "Are you aware that Claude Pepper is known all over Washington as a shameless extrovert?" fast-talking George Smathers is said to have whispered to Florida rural audiences. "Not only that, but this man is reliably reported to practice nepotism with his sister-in-law, and he has a sister who was once a thespian in wicked New York. Worst of all, it is an established fact that Mr. Pepper before his marriage habitually practiced celibacy." Apparently the "wicked thespian" speech originated in North Florida taverns and railway cars, where the press corps gathered to embellish the day's boring events.[30]

Pepper's critics targeted the candidate's ties with everyone from Paul Robeson to Joseph Stalin. The *Orlando Sentinel* published a photograph of Pepper shaking hands with black voters. Gen. Sumter Lowry, a right-wing war hero from Tampa, crisscrossed the state delivering speeches and writing editorials warning Americans about evil pillars of communism and integration and their red offspring, the University of Florida and Claude Pepper. The American Medical Association targeted Pepper for his support of nationalized health insurance. Smathers applauded Lowry's vision of a communist nightmare and urged the United States to consider putting "Reds under surveillance."[31]

Senator's Pepper's archnemesis, Ed Ball, lived for this moment. In the previous decade, the rivals had clashed over U.S. government policies toward war profiteers. Ball's duPont container manufacturing businesses recorded impressive gains and profits during the war years. In January 1944, Senator Pepper visited the Breakers Hotel in Palm Beach, owned by the duPont trust. The U.S. Army had turned a section of the luxury hotel into a wartime convalescent hospital. Pepper recorded in his diary, "Learning that the owners of the golf course were insistent that the soldiers could not get more than two feet off the hotel walks, I advised that the golf course be taken over." Ball went ballistic over what was verified as a false allegation. "Nothing ever got Mr. Ball's blood boiling quicker than this erroneous statement," remembered a close associate.[32]

George Smathers swore that it was Ed Ball and not his campaign staff that smeared Pepper with the most vicious allegations. Ball's associate Dan Crisp published and disseminated a pamphlet, *The Red Record of Claude Pepper*. "Ball," recollected Smathers, "hated Claude Pepper. He was the most conservative man I ever knew."[33]

Ball was also plotting a takeover of the bankrupt Florida East Coast Railway. Senator Pepper's Finance committee stood in his way. On populist and personal principles, Pepper bitterly opposed Ball and his interests from acquiring the railway. Pepper won Round 1, but Ball never forgave or forgot the imbroglio. By 1950, wrote historian Tracy E. Danese, "Ball's whole sense of political purpose was focused on Pepper." When asked how Ball influenced the election, Jake Belin, who was a witness to the campaign, explained the game plan: "Ball had press, he had people, he had newspapers, he had people going out and doing things, for instance getting and running the photographs [of Pepper] at dinner with Stalin and Paul Robeson."[34]

On primary day, Smathers claimed 55 percent of the vote, smashing Pepper. In 1955, Pepper and Ball ran into one another in Tallahassee. Pepper reached out to his adversary, commenting, "Ed, we are growing old. We should stop fighting." Ball snapped back, "You threw a brick at me without cause and I threw one at you." Pepper countered that Ball had thrown the first brick in 1944, "without cause."[35]

Caldwell Returns to Florida: The 1950s

After serving two years as director of the Federal Civil Defense Administration, Caldwell resigned. His tenure had not been personally or professionally satisfying. Friends and critics never understood why he returned to Washington, a place that awakened painful memories. His views toward race and national defense, largely understood and accepted in Florida and the South, incited outbursts of anger, criticism, and ridicule. The Caldwells returned to Tallahassee and their beloved Harwood. Millard resumed practice at his old law firm as well as becoming a bank president.

Caldwell's most unusual clients may have been the Seminole and Miccosukee tribes. Native Americans, like corporate leaders and political bosses, recognized that Millard Caldwell, Esq., was a powerful, well-placed lawyer. Long standing issues ranging from language to tribal membership to reservation politics separated the Miccosukees from the Seminoles. In the 1950s, the Miccosukees were considered a "segment" of the larger Seminole Nation. The Seminoles received federal recognition in 1957, a "victory" that resulted in a further schism between the two Native tribes, especially when the Seminoles received 200,000 acres of Everglades land. The Miccosukee sought federal recognition in 1959, a time of deteriorating relations between the U.S. and Native Americans. "Truth being sometimes stranger than fiction," reflected a journalist writing for *Indian Country Today*, "the Miccosukees' relatively obscure story ties them to Fidel Castro's split with the American government in a brilliant moment of American political strategizing." Miccosukee Chief Buffalo Tiger threatened to take his case to the World Court in the Hague. He even negotiated with Spanish and British diplomats, insisting that his people had been promised land under colonial treaties. The ultimate trump card was sent to Havana, a "buckskins declaration" written on deerskins. Fidel invited the Miccosukee delegation to the 26 July celebration in Havana. The eleven-member delegation included Buffalo Tiger and Mad Dog Anderson. Cuba became the first nation to recognize Miccosukee sovereignty. Governor LeRoy Collins and American diplomats were not pleased by such actions. Florida threatened to reconsider the lease of 200,000 acres in the Everglades. "My people will go on the warpath if we get cheated of our lands," vowed Buffalo Tiger. "We mean business." He added that "the first scalp taken" would be that of Millard Caldwell, who once represented the Miccosukee, but had fallen out of favor because of legal fees and politics![36]

National and statewide candidates also sought Caldwell's blessings throughout the 1950s. In the 1952 election, Caldwell preferred Republican Dwight Eisenhower to Democrat Adlai Stevenson. But the U.S. Supreme Court's *Brown v. Topeka School Board* decision in 1954 outraged Caldwell, dulling his admiration for Ike, who had nominated Earl Warren to the court. Years later he told an audience that state governors once enjoyed great powers, such as the power to call out the National Guard. "At least that was the power before Eisenhower won the battle of Little Rock."[37]

Disillusioned by Ike, Caldwell endorsed Stevenson as his preferred Democratic candidate in the 1956 race. In doing so, he snubbed his fellow Tennessean, U.S. Senator Estes Kefauver, whom many considered the frontrunner. An angry Kefauver called Caldwell "a violent segregationist." Caldwell claimed that he did not "see any profit in choosing a man who cannot be nominated and who cannot be elected." Caldwell's name, editorialized the *Lakeland Ledger,* "is one that means granite stability in the minds of Floridians," and his approval of Stevenson represented "a very influential blessing."[38]

To appear more dignified, Kefauver appeared without his trademark apparel—the coonskin hat. The popularity of the new Disney television show, *Davy Crockett,* had practically made the hapless raccoon an endangered species. The Florida primary was critical for both candidates. In Tampa, the candidates smoked cigars, while walking a tightrope trying to appear moderate on the issue of the Supreme Court's *Brown* decision, but not too liberal. Caldwell was quoted from a newspaper that labeled the Tennessean an "integrationist" and "a sycophant of the Negro vote." Stevenson won the Florida primary by twelve thousand votes. A petulant Kefauver blamed Caldwell for "losing my head" in Florida, charging that his former friend had conducted a "smear and smile" campaign. Nor was Stevenson pleased with Caldwell. In St. Petersburg, Caldwell introduced Stevenson at a rally at Williams Park. Stevenson did not hear, or claimed he did not hear, Caldwell applauding the candidate for his commitment to "white supremacy" and "interposition." Stevenson disavowed Caldwell's remarks.[39]

In the 1956 Florida gubernatorial race, Caldwell held little affection for Charley Johns, a small-minded state legislator from Starke and president of the senate who became governor in 1954 following the death of Governor Dan McCarty. Not even Johns's shortcomings could persuade Caldwell to endorse LeRoy Collins. Their relationship had long ago soured since Collins had helped steer the governor's Minimum Foundation Program through the 1947 Legislature. Governor Caldwell regarded Collins as "ambitious." The schism was personal and political. "The physical proximity of Caldwell and Collins in Tallahassee," wrote biographer Tom Wagy, "exacerbated the tensions between them. Socially, Caldwell . . . did not enjoy the local status of Collins, a hometown boy." Professionally, Caldwell and Collins practiced law at Tallahassee's two most powerful law firms. In 1950, one of Caldwell's law partners had run against State Senator Collins in what locals thought was a spiteful campaign.[40]

Increasingly, Millard Caldwell played the role of an Old Testament prophet, decrying the moral and political climate. He continued his attack line, dispirited by "an endangered" Southern way of life under attack by groups and movements "bent upon a new social order and a paternalistic form of government." The former governor championed a hard line in the Cold War, telling University of Florida students in 1953, "No responsible person, not even the remnants of isolationists, suggests the possibility of reaching acceptable accord with Communism." In 1956, he proclaimed, "I am not in favor of new industry in Florida. I don't believe Florida needs industry and I think the state's future will be endangered by it." He added, "I'd just as soon live in Pittsburgh." In the same speech, he hurled another thunderbolt, lecturing that football teams had no place at the modern university. One newspaper mocked Caldwell as preferring "a plantation economy unsullied by wicked industrial enterprises." Caldwell preferred the old to the new, agreeing in 1958 to chair a committee charged with writing guidelines for the historic preservation of Tallahassee's oldest homes.[41]

The Gubernatorial Race: 1960

Throughout 1958 and early 1959, Florida newspapers speculated as to when Caldwell would announce his candidacy for governor. The Florida constitution prohibited governors from succeeding themselves but permitted individuals to serve nonconsecutive terms. "Millard Caldwell has maneuvered himself into an advantageous position in the 1960 sweepstakes for governor," opined one paper. As Governor LeRoy Collins gradually and then dramatically unloosed the ball and chain of segregation and pleaded for "moral simple justice," Caldwell seethed. Asked in 1976 if he had mellowed toward LeRoy Collins, he replied, "I have not changed my mind on the destructive forces behind desegregation. . . . I don't want to say an unkind word against Governor Collins, but we approached the question from diametrically opposite poles."[42]

Caldwell disappointed supporters and friends when he announced that he would not seek the governorship. He compared becoming governor again the equivalent of "eating yesterday's poached eggs." He added that if he sought office again, it would be the state supreme court. "Strange as it may seem," he remarked with a side of sarcasm, "I much prefer living in our 130-year-old farmhouse to the occupancy of the imitation Hermitage (the governor's mansion)."[43]

The *Tampa Tribune,* in a penetrating editorial about Caldwell's decision not to run for governor, applauded his "wise" decision. "The man . . . has presence," the paper marveled. "His ruggedness of manner is impressive even when his judgment is not." But the *Tribune,* long a supporter, announced a parting of ways. "Increasingly in recent years, he has shown a reluctance to recognize the new Florida. . . . In the great issue of preserving public schools, he has scolded the 'moderates' . . . his public speeches on issues of the day have been more critical than constructive." The paper noted that Caldwell had hosted a political rally in West Florida featuring Arkansas governor Orval Faubus, a hardline segregationist. The decade of the Sixties had only begun, and Caldwell was well suited and situated for the role of Jeremiah.[44]

In January 1960, a headline appeared, announcing with relief, "Segregation No Issue in Governor Campaign." Events and issues quickly made the headline obsolete. The 1960 gubernatorial election turned into, in the words of journalist Martin Dyckman, "a referendum on racial moderation." Depending upon one's perspective and standing, racial moderation meant progress or surrender.[45]

Traditionally, sitting governors took a stand of neutrality regarding their successors. The 1960 race climaxed with a runoff between two contrasting candidates. C. Farris Bryant, a World War II veteran and Marion County state legislator, served two terms as speaker of the Florida House of Representatives. In 1957, he introduced the interposition resolution to close Florida's public schools as a last-ditch defense against federal authority. He challenged Collins's policies and his vision of Florida and the South. Bryant boldly and simply defined his platform: "I am a firm believer in firm segregation." Bryant's opponent, Doyle E. Carlton Jr., was the son of Governor Doyle Carlton. A sixth-generation Floridian raised in Tampa, he supported Collins on many issues. He characterized himself as a "moderate integrationist," setting up a clash over race and the future of Florida, as well as a test of wills of the two wings of Florida's Democratic Party. In a televised debate, Carlton announced that if all legal appeals had been exhausted, he would allow his child to remain in an integrated school. Bryant defiantly insisted he would withdraw his child in such circumstances.[46]

Unrepentant and unbowed, Caldwell led conservative Democrats who felt they were fighting a last stand to save the state from northern meddlers, federal bureaucrats, and a "namby-pamby cult of no conviction." But the 1960 election also reignited decades-old hard and hurt feelings between Tallahassee's quarreling neighbors: Millard Caldwell and LeRoy Collins. The champion of the moderate wing of the party, Collins felt emboldened by the growth of South Florida. When asked to assess the candidates early in the campaign, Caldwell confessed that he could see little difference among them. He retorted, "Most of these gentlemen are moderate in their views, and I am not much of a one for moderates." He added, "A moderate is one who stands for things that are not acceptable in the South." Collins retorted that this must mean that Caldwell was "immoderate."[47]

Four days before the runoff election, Caldwell endorsed Bryant in a televised address, emphasizing Carlton's soft stance against segregation, whereas "Bryant has long been tough in his opposition to integration." Collins answered Caldwell's call and endorsed Carlton, who called the "Bryant-Caldwell alliance . . . a perfect example of compounded bigotry, prejudice, retrogression, and pork barreling." Bryant trounced Carlton, becoming governor in January 1961. Despite his campaign rhetoric, Bryant, wrote the *New York Times* decades later, was "not a demagogue or an obstructionist in the mold of Gov. George C. Wallace of Alabama." Bryant once confessed "The less said about segregation, the better. To talk about it merely incites people and doesn't solve the problem."[48]

Justice Caldwell

Shortly after Bryant's inauguration, Florida Supreme Court Justice T. Frank Hobson stepped down from the bench. The new governor quickly appointed Millard Caldwell to succeed Hobson. Caldwell became the fourth Florida governor to serve on the esteemed court, but the others had been on the court before assuming the governor's office.[49]

"Gov. Caldwell's conservatism in recent years has been extreme, even crusty," noted the *St. Petersburg Times*. Yet the paper supported the ex-governor, maintaining that his high standards of integrity assured a successful appointment. Caldwell's alma mater, the University of Virginia Law School, noted his appointment to the Florida Supreme Court. "The Tennessee native," the school newspaper pointed out, "is an outspoken conservative and critic of the United States Supreme Court." Governor Bryant defined Caldwell as "a conservative in the true Southern tradition," adding that the former governor "did not seek the job. The job sought the man." After his swearing in oath, Caldwell, age sixty-five, announced that he would run for a full six-year term in May.[50]

Justice Caldwell had found a new forum to vent his disillusionment. He assailed the U.S. Supreme Court's pandering to "left wingers and minorities," as well as its "judicial tyranny." He suggested the high court consider "good country lawyers" as replacements. In an oft quoted address, Caldwell channeled his inner Tacitus and Cicero, comparing 1960s America with the Roman Republic. "The Roman Republic," Caldwell opined, "the foremost power of its day had reached its zenith . . . its rulers were intolerant of restraint, indifferent to the demands of the middle class, and contemptuous of the Constitution . . . its citizens grown slick and fat, careless of their rights, and fallen prey to ruthless politicians who craved more and even more power and riches." On another occasion, he lectured that "Roosevelt changed the character of government." The president, explained the justice, "did what the leaders of Rome and Persia did to their people—robbing them of their independence and willingness to work for a living."[51]

"Millard Fillmore Caldwell's 1962 appointment to the Florida Supreme Court," argue two historians of that judicial body, "stood in contrast to those of his immediate three predecessors, E. Harris Drew, B. Campbell Thornal, and Stephen C. O'Connell." In addition to the maelstrom of social and cultural issues that had taken place in the years preceding 1962, Canter Brown Jr. and Walter Manley point out that those predecessors had represented examples each of a "tale of talented but poor young men who had struggled in south Florida to emerge able to offer contributions through public service. Caldwell harkened back to the days when wealthy middle and west Florida planters pursued the law as a kind of noblesse oblige." The portrait of Caldwell rings true, but class and privilege are not destiny. State and federal courts bear many examples of individuals from privileged backgrounds who have become champions of the under-classes.[52]

Justice Caldwell detested the cultural excesses and values of the 1960s that he watched on television, read about in the newspapers, and observed on Tallahassee's college campuses. As student protests engulfed Florida A & M and Florida State University Caldwell complained to governor-elect Bryant about "the ultra-left-wing liberalism" sweeping Tallahassee and Gainesville, blaming Governor Collins's failure to confront the protestors, and the weak leadership of the liberal campus leaders. He pleaded for Bryant to "not tolerate the pinks as faculty or students." Meanwhile, the Legislature's notorious Johns Committee purged gay and lesbian students and faculty. The justice reveled in the role as "Florida's Mr. Conservative."[53]

The justice also disapproved of the tampering of institutions that he had helped found. In 1962, Caldwell wrote to the director of the Southern Regional Education Board, expressing outrage at the organization's acceptance of federal aid. He informed Winfred Godwin, "The Regional program was conceived as a vehicle for a do-it-ourselves effort-as a means of escaping that which you now advocate. . . . I am sorry to see it."[54]

Justice Caldwell addressed the annual meeting of the Association of American Physicians and Surgeons in October 1965. In a much-quoted speech, he took no prisoners. In one sentence, he summarized his seething discontent over the direction of law and society. "The Negroes are happy in the belief that the Brown decision established superior rights for them over the majority; the criminals are happy with the Mallory and Escobedo decisions because of the great advantage gained over the law enforcement officers and society in general; the communists thoroughly approve the . . . cases which insure their right to infiltrate the legal profession and the schools."[55]

Skillfully weaving anger, even revulsion, with a resurgent federal government, Justice Caldwell was a popular after-dinner speaker. "I used to be in the cattle business," he told the Florida Cattlemen's Convention in 1964. "I was in the cattle business when all we had to do was outguess the weather, outguess the ticks and the screwworms and outguess the market." Combining self-deprecation and political oratory, Caldwell had the audience howling when he took aim at old and new enemies: "But when it became necessary to outguess the progeny of Henry Wallace in the Department of Agriculture and the political manipulation in the State Department who were determined to open our doors to the ragged pants nations and their skinny cows, I decided it was time to leave the cow business to the pros."[56]

Caldwell's work ethic as a Supreme Court justice mirrored his philosophy as a gentleman planter and governor. He was not a complicated man in thought, deed, or expression. Guided by core values, Caldwell was known for his decisiveness and precision. Caldwell, remarked fellow justice Stephen C. O'Connell, "prided himself on the fact that most of his decisions were one page." He enjoyed driving his vintage Rolls Royce around town and spending two-hour lunches at the Capital City Country Club. As Caldwell often reminded young colleagues and older associates, "If you can't make a living practicing law from nine to noon and two to five, you shouldn't be a lawyer."[57]

One of Caldwell's closest friends was Bonnie Kaslo "B. K." Roberts. Born into poverty and raised in Sopchoppy (Wakulla County), Roberts, through force of personality, intellect, and friendships, grew wealthy from investments. Roberts's uncle, Angus Morrison, served as the longtime sheriff of Wakulla County, a critical ally in Ball's hotel and real estate dealings along Wakulla Springs. Roberts's shrewd legal maneuverings protected Ball's assets in a divorce settlement. Another close friend, Governor Fuller Warren appointed Roberts to the Florida Supreme Court. B. K. later blustered that he served as Ball's personal attorney while also serving on the court. Roberts was unusually close to legislators—critics charged that he was way too intimate. In many ways, Roberts played the role of "fixer," the go-to person when one needed advice for boardroom discretions and bedroom indiscretions.[58]

For every Roberts's appropriation, appointment, or simple favor, opponents complained of the unfair playing field. In 1965, at the urging of Roberts, Florida State University established a law school. The decision wrought consequences, in this case the closing of the newly opened law school at Florida A&M. Caught in the crossfire was Virgil Darnell Hawkins, a native of Okahumpka in Lake County. While teaching at Bethune-Cookman College in 1949, he applied for admission to the University of Florida Law School. A brilliant student, he was denied admission because of his color. He challenged the decision and won. To mollify the agitator, the legislature created a separate law school at Florida A&M, but Hawkins refused to enroll. Nine years of legal battles ended in 1958. The University of Florida agreed to admit black students to its law school *if* Hawkins withdrew his application. Sadly, despite several U.S. Supreme Court decisions, Hawkins was never admitted. Hawkins, however, paved the way for the next generation.[59]

If Justice Caldwell's critics hoped that his age might moderate his judicial outlook or soften his tongue, they were mistaken. Like Horatius at the gate, Caldwell attempted to arrest the encroaching powers of the federal government, precisely when the Warren Court and Congress struck down many pillars of the Old and New South and rural Florida: (*Baker v. Carr* (1962), one person-one vote; the Voting Rights Acts; and *Gideon v. Wainwright* (1963), the right to counsel. Legal scholar Mary E. Adkins summarized, "Justice Caldwell struggled to understand or recognize the U.S. Supreme Court and its "new Law of the Land." He supported the constitutionality of mandatory school prayer and Bible reading in public schools. "We are sensible of the extent to which the sophistries of agnosticism have gained credence," began Caldwell in his written opinion in the 1962 case, *Chamberlin, et al. v. Dade County Board of Public Instruction.* In *McLaughlin v. Florida* (1964), Justice Caldwell wrote a blistering opinion upholding a statute prohibiting interracial cohabitation. Anti-miscegenation laws were as old as Florida statehood. In 1964, the U.S Supreme Court reversed a Florida Supreme Court decision approving Bible reading and required prayers in Florida public schools. Justice Caldwell had written the Florida court's opinion, and upon hearing of the reversal, remarked it was "not surprising." In *Loving v. Virginia* (1938), the U.S. Supreme Court unanimously overturned laws prohibiting interracial marriage. Caldwell was outraged.[60]

Caldwell admired J. Stanley Marshall, the president of Florida State University between 1969 and 1976. His admiration was not widely shared on the campus, where students and faculty clashed with Marshall, a political and social conservative. Soon after taking the reins of FSU, Marshall spearheaded a legal effort to ban the Students for a Democratic Society (SDS) from campus. Caldwell applauded Marshall's efforts to quell the liberal tide. In 1987, Marshall founded the James Madison Institute, a conservative think tank in Tallahassee.[61]

The Carswell and Cross-State Barge Fiascos: 1969–1970

When Justice Caldwell stepped down from the bench in January 1969, he realized that his four-decade long career as a public servant had ended. No other Floridian had ever served in all three branches of Florida government: as governor, state legislator, and the State Supreme Court. He also served as a U.S. congressman, never losing an election in a half century of service.

Just months after his retirement, he became embroiled in the confirmation hearings of a trusted friend and law associate. In January 1970, President Richard Nixon nominated a Tallahassee judge, G. Harrold Carswell to the U.S. Supreme Court. Nixon had triumphed in the 1968 presidential election, in part because of his brilliantly orchestrated "Southern strategy." Kevin Phillips, author of *The Emerging Republican Majority,* convinced the president that the political stars had aligned, creating a historic opportunity for the GOP to invade and divide the South's white voters. The irony of the Party of Lincoln triumphant in the South was not lost on Nixon. A frightening spike in crime emboldened the Republican message, as did the unsettling desegregation of southern schools.[62]

President Nixon vowed to appoint southern conservative judges to blunt the Warren Court's overreach. To deliver his promise, Nixon nominated Federal Judge Clement Furman Haynsworth, a longtime South Carolinian, to become associate justice on the U.S. Supreme Court. But Senate Democrats assailed Haynsworth's record on civil rights and rejected the nominee.[63]

Furious, President Nixon began the search for another nominee. On 18 December 1969 a *St. Petersburg Times'* headline hinted, "Nixon Said Eying Carswell for High Court." Attorney General John Mitchell took control of the vetting, promising that Carswell was a choir boy. No Floridian had ever served on the U.S. Supreme Court, and Carswell seemed, in the words of a contemporary Broadway musical, "a shoo-in."

Born in Georgia in 1919, Carswell had deep roots in the Peach State. A veteran of WWII, Lt. Carswell returned to Georgia, resumed his studies, and practiced law. He ran unsuccessfully for the Georgia legislature and governor's office. In 1948, the Carswells moved to Florida. In Tallahassee, he joined a law firm that included future governor LeRoy Collins. President Eisenhower appointed Carswell judge of the Florida Northern District in 1958, and President Nixon elevated him to a judge on the U.S. Court of Appeals for the Fifth Circuit.

A *St. Petersburg Times* headline predicted, "Confirmation Appears Certain." Critics attacked Carswell for his "mediocre" judicial record as well as his persistent support of segregation. Both Millard Caldwell and LeRoy

Collins endorsed Carswell's nomination. Collins testified that Carswell was neither a racist nor segregationist.

Old and new demons awaited Carswell. The decades of the 1960s and '70s, an era of war, civil rights, the dawn of environmental awareness, and campus activism, smashed the comfortable worlds of Carswell and Caldwell. The new era demanded a reckoning with hurtful rhetoric and deeds. An investigative reporter discovered a speech delivered by Carswell in 1948 in which he told an American Legion audience, "Segregation of the races is proper and the only practical and correct way of life in our states." He added, with emphasis, "I yield to no man, as a fellow candidate or as a fellow citizen, the firm vigorous belief in the principles of white supremacy."[64]

A Tallahassee golf course became an unlikely setting for a Supreme Court controversy. For decades, the Tallahassee Municipal Golf Course and its large ballroom and dance floor had functioned as Tallahassee's social center. The 205-acre golf course and buildings were leased from the city for one dollar a year for ninety-nine years. The golf course was open to "any acceptable person," but in 1956, African Americans protested the club's "whites only" policies. The following year, the golf course was renamed the Capital City Country Club and reorganized as a "for-profit" organization. Carswell served as the "incorporator" of the club. Critics charged that the transfer was a charade, an all-too familiar legal maneuver to avoid desegregation.[65]

Critics had long waited to grill this judicial nominee. The Rev. C. K. Steele, a civil rights hero in Tallahassee, testified that Judge Carswell exuded southern charm with equal doses of obstructionism and racism. Betty Friedan contended, "Racism and sexism often go hand in hand." Prominent law professors questioned Carswell's worthiness, citing a high number of overturned opinions. When nine FSU law school professors urged President Nixon to withdraw Carswell's name and nominate a "truly distinguished Southern jurist," the school's president and trustees expressed outrage. One critic snidely pointed out that Carswell was a "dull graduate of the third best law school in the state of Georgia." U.S. Senator

Roman Hruska (R-Nebraska) defended Carswell, pointing out, "Even if he were mediocre, there are a lot of mediocre judges and people and lawyers, and they are entitled to a little representation, aren't they?" On 8 April 1970, the U.S. Senate rejected Carswell 51 to 45.[66]

Crestfallen, a determined Carswell rebounded, announcing that he was a candidate for the 1970 U.S. Senate seat. He lost the nomination to Congressman William Cramer, who in turn was defeated by upstart Walkin' Lawton Chiles. In 1976, Harrold Carswell suffered more humiliation when he was arrested and convicted of battery after propositioning an undercover police officer at a men's room in the Northwood Mall in Tallahassee. His old friend and colleague, Millard Caldwell, was crushed. Caldwell, like many Americans of his generation, could not fathom that a trusted friend could be a homosexual. Curiously and improbably, Carswell's life served as a touchstone of the era's passions and prejudices.[67]

Carswell symbolized the speed and force of change that the decades of the 1960s and 1970s wrought upon Florida. When asked who won the 1960s culture wars, historians often answer: "The Republican Party!" The decade of the 1960s alternately diminished and emboldened the Republican Party of Florida. Floridians narrowly favored Republican Richard Nixon over John Kennedy in 1960. Four years later, Lyndon Johnson defeated the conservative Barry Goldwater by only 43,000 votes. But a new generation of moderate and liberal Democrats representing growing urban districts in Central and South Florida entered the Florida legislature and the U.S. Congress.

A new Republican era also took hold in 1966. The Florida Republican Party benefited greatly from the growing unpopularity of President Johnson and the unrest in inner cities and college campuses. Florida was a perfect place for Claude Kirk Jr. His life resembled a combination of rags-to-riches Horatio Alger and Harold Hill, the trombone huckster in *The Music Man*. Growing up in the hardscrabble section of Montgomery, Alabama, he joined the marines at age seventeen at the close of WWII. The GI Bill enabled him to graduate from Emory University and the University of Alabama law school. He joined the stampede to the Sun Belt, moving his family to Florida in 1956. A born salesman, Kirk made a fortune in the insurance business. In 1960, Kirk led the "Democrats for Nixon" Florida committee. Somehow, he won the GOP nomination for governor in 1966. The Democratic Party, wrestling with growth, Vietnam, and a civil rights movement, nominated Miami liberal Democrat Robert King High to run for governor. Kirk became the first Republican to lead the Sunshine State since Ossian B. Hart was elected in 1872. Millard Caldwell did not join the exodus from the Democratic Party to the GOP. Even though he and many North Florida Democrats loathed the party's nominee, they did not bolt.[68]

Governor Claude Kirk took his oath of office from Chief Justice Caldwell in January 1967. No modern gubernatorial candidate had ever campaigned so passionately for the black vote as High, who vigorously endorsed integration and supported the Civil Rights acts. Caldwell disapproved of Kirk and his playboy image. Hours after taking his oath of office, the new governor appeared at his inaugural ball with a thirty-three-year-old blonde, introduced simply as Madame X. In a 1975 interview, Caldwell summarized his opinion of Governor Kirk by stating, "Claude was never elected; the other chap was defeated." Caldwell noted that while he offered advice to Kirk, "He did not follow it. I gave him hell . . . and I told him at the time that he was trying to get himself beat."[69]

"Claudius Maximus," as the press dubbed Kirk, proved a better campaigner and showman than governor and party leader. He created his own security force, flirted with Nixon to become his running mate in 1968, and threatened to fire school principals who cooperated with federal officials. His missteps led to a bitter 1968 state teachers' strike. His biographer chose a perfect subtitle: "The Politics of Confrontation."[70]

Governor Kirk was unpredictable, witnessed by his growing anxiety over the Cross-Florida Barge Canal. The ambitious proposal to build a canal from Jacksonville to the Gulf Coast had divided Floridians for generations. President Johnson, eager to add Florida to his electoral quiver, jumpstarted the project in 1964. Caldwell and his North Florida neighbors had long supported the pork-barrel project. Congressman Caldwell had even applauded President Roosevelt's approval of the project in 1935, describing it as "the outstanding achievement of the century." The 1930s boondoggle found new life with President Johnson, but Governor Kirk found religion—or political fear—in the growing environmental movement, concluding that the concept was as flawed as it was doomed. The retirement of U.S. Senator Spessard Holland in 1970, a longtime protector of the canal, buoyed environmentalists. The story is told that while President Nixon was campaigning in Florida in the Fall of 1970 he noticed a sea of signs protesting the canal. "There is opposition to your canal," remarked the president. Kirk quipped, "No, Mr. President, not my canal, but *your* canal!" President Nixon killed the canal with an executive order in 1971.[71]

5

CONCLUSION

Who Belongs on the Pedestal?

Caldwell enjoyed his status as Florida's oldest surviving chief executive. He still commanded attention and respect, evident in his appearance before the first organizational session of the 1977–78 Florida Constitution Revision Commission. The esteemed jurist and future president of Florida State University Talbot "Sandy" D'Alemberte served as chair of the body. In his introduction, he spoke with a sense of pride knowing that "most of the members were probably filled with a sense of historic purpose, having been brought together for a task unique in the nation." The mood of euphoria and optimism, noted D'Alemberte, "was somewhat shattered by a speech . . . by Millard Caldwell, who said that the advice given to the Commission which met in 1968 was that it 'should meet, organize, adjourn sine die, and go home.'" Then and in 1977 Caldwell pleaded for the commission not to make any changes to the existing constitution. The eighty-year-old former governor and justice hectored the committee to repeal public employee collective bargaining. "I suspect the greatest disaster in all of Florida's history was its recent capture by the labor unions," he complained. Caldwell also characterized the notions of financial disclosure and government in the sunshine as "silly."[1]

He treasured his last years at the Harwood plantation, where he preferred driving an old tractor to his vintage Rolls Royce. "I practice law in the morning," he told a reporter in 1977, "but in the afternoon, I work for

Willie." Willie Laster worked for the Caldwell family, in charge of the vegetable garden. Nostalgically, the man who served as congressman, governor, state supreme court justice, and director of a powerful federal agency, confided that his happiest days were spent in the state legislature. "I was an obstructionist, and that probably isn't good. But all my efforts were against serious wrongs, and I loved the fights." He disapproved of Florida governors jetting around the state and conducting state business at all hours. "I don't think that in four years I was in the mansion I had ten calls at night about business. . . . I personally preferred to do all the business in the office during office hours and then live at home." He drew great satisfaction in his service. "So far as I know, no breath of scandal touched any of my administration people."[2]

Millard Fillmore Caldwell died 23 October 1984 at age eighty-seven. Allen Morris praised his friend as "a sturdy oak of Florida government." The *Tallahassee Democrat's* Malcolm Johnson, who first observed the thirty-four-year-old legislator in 1931, believed he was "the best governor we've had in my lifetime." The *New York Times* noted he was a "conservative Democrat." Justice Stephen O'Connell, who had served with Caldwell on the Florida Supreme Court, characterized Caldwell as a "grand gentleman . . . a tall, erect, forceful individual in appearance as well as in manner." In the 1944 gubernatorial race, Caldwell had upset Ernest Graham to secure the Democratic Party's nomination. Bob Graham, Ernest's son, served as Florida's governor at the time of Caldwell's death. Mary Harwood Caldwell passed away in 1986. The Caldwell's two daughters, Sally McCord and Susan Cavanaugh, died in 2003 and 2013.[3]

In July 1986, the Caldwell plantation home was carefully jacked up, loaded on truck beds, and moved nine miles on the Old Bainbridge Road to Florida State University's College of Law campus. The journey took four days. The home still serves as an academic-office village. The home was donated by Fred and Sally Caldwell McCord.[4]

Assessing Millard Fillmore Caldwell is challenging. In *Julius Caesar*, Shakespeare lionizes "the noblest Roman of them all." Mark Antony reminds Romans of the great man's generosity and empathy: "When the poor have cried, Caesar hath wept. Ambition should be made of sterner stuff." Glaringly absent from Caldwell's virtues were empathy and compassion. One searches in vain for his thoughts or positive actions on the plight and suffering of Florida's poorest citizens.

How shall we judge the whole life of Caldwell? Like Jacob Marley, the shackles and ghosts of the past haunt Caldwell. Oblivious and even obstinate, he challenged at every turn one of the great historical moments and movements in American history: the civil rights revolution. If he were better known, protestors would be chiseling away his nameplate from the humdrum Caldwell building.

From the perspective of 2019, Millard Caldwell's dedicated record of service is tar-brushed by his obstinacy over issues of race and change. Yet when he left office in 1949, he was regarded as one of Florida's great governors, in large part because of his service as a wartime governor and as the architect of the Minimum Foundation Program. Newspapers generally hailed Caldwell's exit. "Greatness, however," writes Edmund Morris, "requires that leaders who change their times be seen to change themselves, or at least embody great ideals."[5]

Should Millard Caldwell's life's work be distilled down, revealing only the spirits of racism? Should we not judge a human's lifespan in its entirety? In 2017, I wrote a column about Caldwell in the *Tampa Bay Times*. I concluded that evaluating Caldwell "is complicated." An angry reader wrote a letter to the editor, with a damning title, "Not 'Complicated'— He's a Racist." The reader asked, "How is it possible to find sympathy for an outright racist?" The reader raised fair, if uncomfortable, even complicated questions that forced me to rethink my attitudes about leadership and Caldwell.[6]

The questions surrounding Caldwell's life and deeds are timeless and timebound: How shall we measure the character and deeds of a single life? When Caldwell died in 1984, friends and pastors invoked the Book of Ecclesiastes: "Let us now praise famous men and our fathers that begat us. Their glory shall remain forever, and their glory shall not be blotted out."

Is Caldwell's historical reputation redeemable? Should we consider his good deeds: military service, progressive educational reform, a dedicated husband and father, a career without a whiff of scandal, and an unfailing honesty with fellow citizens? Such questions resonate powerfully at a moment when statues and school names of Confederate generals and Spanish explorers are toppled and cursed. Or as the letter to the editor asked, "How is it possible to find sympathy for an outright racist?"[7]

We live in an age of revisionism. Every age is whiplashed by the winds of revisionism. Consider Napoleon Bonaparte Broward, Florida governor. Once praised as a Cuban freedom fighter and a "fighting Democrat" and progressive, Broward is now depicted as an environmental villain for draining the Everglades and a nativist and racist for advocating colonization of Florida's black population. A recent newspaper headline queried, "Is Broward named for a racist?" Broward County commissioners voted to remove the namesake statue from the courthouse.[8]

Each generation deserves its own heroes. In 1864, the U.S. Congress invited the states to select two persons "illustrious for their historic renown or distinguished civic or military service." In bronze and marble, states began to dispatch favorite sons (and occasional daughters) to the Capitol's Statuary Hall. From the beloved (Oklahoma's Will Rogers), to the distant (Hawaii's King Kamehameha), to the obscure (Arkansas's Uriah Rose), the august hall and its stately rotunda function as an American Pantheon and Olympus.[9]

In 1914, Florida proudly dedicated a bronze statue of Dr. John Gorrie, "the almost sacred" Apalachicola physician who in 1851 patented a "machine for the artificial production of ice." Caldwell, who disapproved of air-conditioning, blamed Gorrie for the flood of pale and effete Yankees to the Sunshine State.[10]

Recognizing the undying legacy of the "War between the States," Floridians selected Edmund Kirby Smith to stand aside Dr. Gorrie. Officials commissioned sculptor C. A. Pillars to cast a bronze statue of the general. Born in St. Augustine in 1824, the West Point graduate fought valiantly in the Mexican War, twice brevetted for bravery. In 1861, he resigned his commission in the U.S. Army to join the Confederacy. Promoted to the rank of lieutenant general in 1863, Kirby Smith became commander of the Trans-Mississippi Department. In 1865, he was the last highly ranked general to surrender. He spent his final decades teaching at the University of the South in Sewanee, Tennessee.[11]

LeRoy Collins has been called by Martin A. Dyckman, his biographer, "Floridian of His Century." The book's subtitle underscores the salient point: "The Courage of Governor LeRoy Collins." Few historians would challenge that bold assessment. But Collins was not a saint. He supported the efforts of Florida's attorney general to halt Virgil Hawkins's integration of the University of Florida Law School. Collins, however, came to understand the era's injustices, and accepted change. Whereas Collins overcame conventional attitudes to question the prevailing attitudes toward race, Caldwell defiantly clung to his ingrained belief that the races should never marry and rarely mix. Despite differences in their family backgrounds, Collins and Caldwell shared many Southern attitudes toward race relations. Caldwell grew up amid plantations and privilege, circumstances unknown to Collins and Tallahassee's "hominy huskers" and "depot greasers." Collins always possessed a soulful empathy for the downtrodden. As governor, he broke ranks with fellow Democrats and most Floridians. Collins understood and accepted the political costs for his plea for "moral, simple justice." He explained his conversion: "I don't have to get re-elected, but I have to live with myself." He asked Floridians to reconsider the sit-ins and the morality of segregation. "While it may be legally acceptable, it is morally wrong," insisted the governor. "It's something I can't justify in my conscience." Collins also understood Jesus's preaching in Luke 4:24, "No prophet is accepted in his hometown." Or his own state. Collins never held elected office again. But as author Edmund Morris reminds us, "History admires the wise, but elevates the brave."[12]

Who belongs on the pedestal? In 2017, the Florida Legislature voted to exile Edmund Kirby Smith from Statuary Hall. A Republican-dominated Florida Legislature voted to replace a Confederate general with Mary McLeod Bethune; the fifteenth child of former slaves, Bethune dedicated her life to education and the uplift of African Americans. President

Truman appointed her to the National Defense Commission, where she served under director Millard Caldwell. She was a confidante to Eleanor Roosevelt. A vexing issue remains: What to do with a controversial bronze statue without a home? In 2018–19, Lake County commissioners agreed to house the statue in Tavares's stately courthouse where the Historical Museum is housed. But long festering issues arose. Lake County is still grappling with the legacy of the Groveland Four and the conduct of its notorious sheriff, Willis McCall. Despite mounting opposition from citizens, many of whom pointed out that Edmund Kirby Smith lacked any association with Lake County, the commission was not moved. Amidst the debate, county commissioners voted to elevate Mabel Norris Reese to the Lake County Women's Hall of Fame. Reese owned the *Mount Dora Topic*, and guided the newspaper's revelations of racial injustice in the 1940s and 1940s.[13]

Millard Caldwell's reputation has long been in the crosshairs of history. In 1967, Springtime Tallahassee debuted. The celebration paid homage to the Capital City, at a time when the Legislature was considering moving the capital to Orlando. The celebration, organized by Tallahassee's first families, venerated the past. Amid the dissonance of the Sixties, a time when it seemed America was spinning apart in violence and protest, Millard Caldwell led the first Springtime Tallahassee parade. Bedecked as General Jackson, Caldwell rode his mount in a tribute that surely would have pleased Old Hickory. Indeed, Jackson and Caldwell shared many traits and qualities: Tall and commanding, they flashed signs of anger when opponents challenged their honor and character. One could easily imagine Millard dueling with riffraff who dared dishonor his beloved wife, Mary. Frontiersmen, Tennesseans, and Democrats, their historical reputations have been sullied because of Jackson's hatred of Indians and defense of slavery and Caldwell's racism and obstinacy.

"Few presidents have been as revered and vilified as Andrew Jackson," writes historian and biographer John Belohlavek. Considering Jackson's attitude and actions toward Native Americans and African Americans, should he be revered or reviled? Should we pull down all the statues and memorials honoring Old Hickory? Recently, vandals defaced his tomb, painting the word "killer" on the monument. As President Obama and Treasury Secretary Lew were leaving office, they recommended that Jackson's portrait be removed from the twenty-dollar bill and replaced with Harriet Tubman. Ironically, Jackson disapproved of paper currency; even more ironic, President Trump, a New Yorker, saved Jackson's place (if not in history, on currency). If Jackson has escaped ignominy, it is largely because of the prevailing feeling that he promoted and championed the expansion of the franchise. He was a self-made man, a democrat who expanded democracy. He fought bravely against Creeks and Seminoles, who ferociously defended their homeland. Old Hickory's triumph at New Orleans over British forces reverberated mightily up and down the young republic as well as the crumbling foundation of Spanish Florida. In comparison to Old Hickory, Caldwell fought to restrict and constrict the voting rights of black Floridians with his spirited defense of the White Primary.[14]

Thomas Jefferson was a patrician of Old Virginia, a plantation owner who sired several children from his slave mistress. Still, historians generally give Jefferson a pass, pointing out his accomplishments (a champion of education, his intellectual creativity and stirring words at critical moments in American history). The stewards of modern Monticello have adapted to the revelations. Today, visitors view Monticello through the lens of slavery and African contributions to life on the mountain.

Jefferson's fellow Virginian, George Washington, may be safe on Mount Rushmore, but in danger elsewhere. Once considered so significant, a historian titled a biography of Washington, *The Indispensable Man*. Washington's overall reputation—his military stature, dignified leadership, an enviable role model as the first president, and the fact that unlike Jefferson, the Father of Our Country freed his slaves—once seemed safe. Washington College honored the great patriot when it was founded in 1749 and in 1870 changed its name to Washington and Lee University out of reverence for Robert E. Lee, who served as college president after the Civil War. But in 2018, "grappling with its complex history," the school took down oil portraits of Generals Washington and Lee, replacing them with portraits of the men in civilian clothes. What is the take-away from such actions? That America should have fought the British with ideas, not bullets?[15]

Perhaps the question of Caldwell's legacy might be better understood *not* by comparisons to Jefferson, Washington, and Jackson, but to his contemporaries? The golden age of the Solid South and southern political mastery occurred during the period between the 1920s and the 1950s. Millard Caldwell shared the stage with Southern giants: J. William Fulbright, Sam Rayburn, Lyndon B. Johnson, Hale Boggs, Wilbur Mills, James Eastland, John C. Stennis, Herman Talmadge, Richard Russell, Walter F. George, L. Mendel Rivers, and Claude Pepper. Statues, schools, and public buildings bear their names and accomplishments. Today, a spirited public backlash questions whether dead white males who were considered heroic in one era should be lionized in another. Every generation deserves its own heroes. And villains. Hero today, gone tomorrow.

New generations of Floridians and historians select new heroes, individuals more attuned to their cultural and political outlooks. Race and gender count more than military and political laurels. Georgian Richard Russell ruled Washington with such power that the U.S. Senate Office building bears his name. How strange is it when U.S. Senator Chuck Schumer, a liberal Democrat and U.S. Senator from New York took the floor to proclaim that it was time to rename the Russell Building in honor of John McCain, a Republican? While Russell was "a towering figure in the Senate of his day, he was nonetheless an avowed opponent of civil rights and the architect of the Southern filibuster that long delayed its passage." Russell and his fellow Georgia senator Walter F. George took great pride in obstructing civil rights legislation, filibustering to block the anti-lynching bill of 1938. Russell earned his nickname, the "senator's senator," a tribute to his mastery of the body's rules and regulations. He employed such mastery to block legislation he opposed. The Law School at Mercer University bore the name Walter F. George, the U.S. Senator from Georgia, 1922–1957. In 2018, Mercer University stripped the name Walter F. George from its law school.[16]

J. William Fulbright represented Arkansas in the U.S. Senate from 1945

to 1974. Fulbright displayed a keen and critical eye in steering U.S. foreign policy. He was one of the first senators to question American involve-
ment in Vietnam. The Fulbright Program honors his legacy. But Fulbright,
like Claude Pepper and young Lyndon Johnson, may have been liberals
in their social outlook, but they defended segregation in order to survive
politically. The ends justify the means. Fulbright, along with other Democrats, filibustered the 1964 Civil Rights Act. U.S. Senator Hugo Black admitted when he was nominated for the U.S. Supreme Court in 1937 that he
had joined the Ku Klux Klan as a young man. West Virginia U.S. Senator
Robert C. Byrd not only joined the Ku Klux Klan as a young man, he held
the office of Exalted Cyclops.[17]

After graduation from Harvard Law School, Claude Pepper taught at
the University of Arkansas, where one of his protégés was J. William Fulbright. They shared a liberal vision of the New South. Pepper's historical
reputation has only soared after his death in 1989. The writer T. D. Allman
argues, "Florida did produce one public figure who, like Ossian Hart in the
previous century, transcended his situation." He explains: "A Southerner
by birth, breeding, and heritage, Senator and later Representative Claude
Pepper (1900–1989) . . . personified the New Deal's hopes and opportunities." But Pepper, like most heroes, lived a complicated life. In the 1937 debate on the Wagner Anti-Lynching Bill, Senator Pepper filibustered, "[T]
he colored race had not and will not vote because in doing to under present circumstances they endanger the supremacy of a race to which God
has committed the destiny of a continent, perhaps the World." The following year, Southern senators announced they had a "solemn covenant" to
block another anti-lynching bill. The Associated Press noted, "The burden
of the speech-making was carried by Senator Pepper, who described the
bill as "a tragic prostitution of the processes of government." Clearly, such
remarks jar with the esteemed congressman who also fought the hard
fight for America's poor and elderly.[18]

In 1974, Congressman Pepper was interviewed by the Southern writer
Jack Bass. Pepper candidly confessed to filibustering against a bill that
would make lynching a federal crime. He explained, "Because I thought

that a Senator from the South had to do that." In other words, to be elected in the South in the 1930s and '40s, the color line was inviolable. The ends justified the means. Only in 2018, following a century of debate, Congress passed legislation making lynching a federal crime.[19]

Exposés make interesting reading but do not answer the question: Who belongs on the pedestal? Revealing that William Fulbright was a racist and Hugo Black a Klansman fail to resolve the dilemma—How do we judge past heroes who have feet of clay? True, judging past heroes by today's standards remains complicated and subject to the dangers of presentism. History demands that we be judicious and fair.

Heroes rise to the occasion. In the 1920s, western Missouri was Klan country. Most politicians joined the Ku Klux Klan out of genuine support or political pragmatism. Harry S. Truman, however, not only refused the invitation of the KKK but called out friends and business associates for their lack of judgment.

A sense of perspective is needed. Until the 1960s and '70s, the press typically shielded politicians—at least friends—from peccadillos ranging from womanizing to alcohol to drugs. U.S. Senator and President John Kennedy would never survive today's "gotcha" press. No one ever accused Millard Caldwell of such indiscretions; indeed, his marriage and affection for Mary Harwell represent a story of devotion and love.[20]

No case better illustrates the new accounting than the Groveland Four. The case, wrote the *Washington Post,* "checked all the boxes for a legal nightmare: It included a false allegation of rape; loaded racial dynamics, a lynch mob; defendants railroaded to death row; and quick-trigger lawmen who may have been out to murder their prisoners." The *Orlando Sentinel* has been especially vigilant in righting the errors of the past, even if this meant exposing the newspaper's racism. Stubbornly, Governor Rick Scott ignored the plaintiff pleas to pardon the Groveland Four, a task which his successor, Governor Ron DeSantis performed.[21]

The City of Tallahassee and FSU have grappled with the thorny issue of old and new heroes. In 2018, Florida State University's "1984"-sounding President's Advisory Panel on University Namings and Recognition recommended to President John Thrasher that Judge B. K. Roberts's name be removed from the academic building at the law school, an institution he helped bring to the campus in 1965. In what can only be called sweet justice, the college of law will be renamed in honor of Virgil Hawkins. FSU has also been embroiled in a decision whether to remove a statue of Francis Eppes VII from the Westcott Plaza. Eppes, a Virginia planter and grandson of Thomas Jefferson, moved to Leon County in 1829. He brought with him African slaves. He purchased additional slaves to build and work on his plantation and estate. He served as mayor of Tallahassee and generously donated the land that became West Florida Seminary, Florida's first state-sponsored university in 1857. In 1947, Governor Caldwell, B. K. Roberts, among others, spearheaded the transformation of Florida State College for Women into today's Florida State University.[22]

Few Floridians bring a personal perspective to the past and present as Diane Roberts, an English professor at Florida State University. Her not-too-distant relatives were close associates of Governor Caldwell; her family lived across Old Bainbridge Road from the First Family. "When my father wanted to buy our land, part of an old pecan plantation, Gov. Caldwell had to attest that daddy was, indeed, a white man," she recalled in her communique. In her 2005 book, *Dream State*, she observed, "Damn, if that isn't Andrew Jackson, Old Hickory himself, riding a bay gelding down Monroe Street in his gold-epauletted coat and cockaded *chapeau bas*, his Ray-Bans and his Rolex." She added, "Andrew Jackson despised Florida. Andrew Jackson lived in Florida less than six months. . . . He practiced genocide."[23]

Understandably, the honor of playing Jackson has lost its luster and its front-row standing. In 2004, Manny González rode Jackson's mount. Roberts quips that Jackson is today "lucky to get a parade slot between Thomas County High School Marching Yellow Jacket Band and the Tallahassee Tumbling Tots."[24]

Arguably, no one could possibly play the oversized Millard Fillmore. But if Caldwell has been reduced to a middling role in Springtime Tallahassee, how is he remembered, if at all, in present day Tallahassee and Florida?

In 1948, state officials dedicated the Caldwell building, located on 107 E. Madison St. The building, constructed in a style described as "masonry vernacular," currently houses the department of Labor, the Department of Economic Opportunity, and the Agency for Workplace Innovation. Caldwell would be perplexed to understand the meaning, need, and point of such an agency. Fittingly, the structure also served as a designated fall-out shelter in case the Soviets fired a nuclear-tipped missile at Tallahassee. Should the building be renamed, and Caldwell's plaque melted down along with the governor's reputation? Caldwell's son-in-law, a Tallahassee banker Fred McCord, spent years lobbying governors to anoint his father-in-law with "Great Floridian" status. In 2014, Governor Rick Scott signed the order.[25]

Born in the horse and buggy era of the 1890s, Caldwell's life spanned the automobile and space age. When Caldwell was born in 1897, Florida's population hovered around a half million residents, most of them born a day's wagon ride from Georgia on Tallahassee's Old Bainbridge Road. When he died, Florida was the fastest growing state in America, with a population of eleven million residents, not counting the surging numbers of tourists and snowbirds.

The last Florida governor born in the nineteenth century, Caldwell was, comfortable in his core beliefs and opinions. He was a man of his times, but he also proved incapable or unwilling to accept more comfortable with the manners, morals, and politics of that century than the twentieth. He railed against the New Deal and the Great Society, student demonstrations and the civil rights revolution, the decline of small farms and rise of Sunbelt cities, environmental regulations and federal agencies.

Millard Caldwell remains vulnerable to caricature as a wealthy planter who preferred the ol' days of Dixie when blacks knew their place and students respected authority. He may have been a Jeffersonian who longed for an America of small towns and yeoman farmers, but he also accepted republican virtues of responsibility, duty, and an educated electorate. Such values deserve to be cherished.

In March 1945, Florida celebrated its state centennial birthday. Governor Caldwell wrote that Florida "is still undeveloped, its destiny still unfulfilled." An unvarnished conservative, he understood conservation, telling Floridians that citizens had an obligation to conserve "our surface and artesian fresh water supply." In 1948, he reflected that his "greatest disappointment as governor was in the area of conservation." A realist, he demanded reform of Florida's public schools, reminding citizens that we should not "tolerate the false economy of starving services essential to our continued growth." In an editorial in the *Gainesville Sun,* Ron Cunningham recommended that Florida Governor Rick Scott aspire to be "a Millard Caldwell visionary." It was Caldwell who said, "In considering all the alternatives available which would advance Florida the most and improve opportunities for the public, I considered that more progress could be made by improving the educational system than any other." It was Caldwell who asked the Legislature to advance higher education by imposing a tax on beer and cigarettes, but for naught. Caldwell then explained, in simple terms, "We are prepared to pay reasonable taxes to build a greater State." He detested the role of money in modern politics. In an age of bombast and verbosity, he was a plainspoken man. In the early 1950s, the *St. Petersburg Times* applauded Caldwell's address to Emory University students. "We have never known him to use four, three or even two words when one would do," beamed an admiring editor.[26]

Caldwell slung insults against a rising tide of liberalism and the resurgence of federal power. But he also witnessed the triumph of his brand of conservatism. At the time of his death, President Ronald Reagan stood on the threshold of reelection, and the Republican Party was making dramatic gains across Florida. Caldwell's beloved Florida Panhandle turned its back on the Democratic Party. Ironically, today's Leon County glows bright blue in a sea of GOP red.

In November 1968, amid the maelstrom of protest and riots, the *Pensacola News-Journal* noted the imminent retirement of Florida's Supreme Court Chief Justice. In a time when heroes seemed to be anti-heroes, the paper editorialized, "Chief Justice Millard Fillmore Caldwell will have completed a career of public service which can serve as a model for all young Americans who wish to dedicate a lifetime to the betterment of their country." Today, such kudos are rare. Even rarer is the message that a lifetime dedicated to public service is ennobling and meritorious. With Caldwell, of course, is the prickly issue of his public service devoted to restricting the electorate and enforcing segregation. The editorial concluded," For this public service effort, he became known as Florida's Mr. Conservative—Mr. Conservative with an acid tongue."[27]

Congressman, governor, and chief justice, Millard Caldwell won eight elections, remained comfortable, confident, and unapologetic about his political beliefs and values. He lacked the qualities of empathy, sympathy, and compassion. He was an exemplary figure, a man of his times, but the times changed, and he was incapable or unwilling to accept and adjust to new ideas, laws, and attitudes.

ACKNOWLEDGMENTS

In the autumn of my life, I feel blessed to acknowledge friends and colleagues who have meant so much to me. I have been extraordinarily fortunate to have so many colleagues that I consider dear friends. Colleagues at the University of South Florida St. Petersburg supported this project. Raymond Arsenault, J. Michael Francis, Chris Meindl, and Thomas Smith inspired me with their work ethic, camaraderie, and high professional standards. It was my good fortune that Robert Kerstein retired to St. Petersburg after many decades of teaching at the University of Tampa. Bob is a first-rate critic. Hugh Tulloch, a retired navy captain, a graduate of Annapolis, and a steadfast auditor, also reviewed this manuscript. Lester Lamon, a UNC classmate, historian, and St. Augustine resident schooled this author on life in eastern Tennessee. David Colburn, another lifelong friend since our UNC days, was never too busy to answer a question about Florida governors.

Before and after my retirement, the Florida Humanities Council offered me refuge and inspiration. My thanks to Ann Henderson, Janine Farver, Barbara Bahr, Laurie Berlin, Alex Buell, Danica Kelley, Lisa Lennox, Jacqui May, Peggy Macdonald, Monica Kile, Brenda O'Hara, Patricia Putnam, Barbara O'Reilley, Keith Simmons, Steve Seibert, Tyler Tarrant, and Jon Wilson.

Andrew Frank and Frederick Rowe Davis, dashing historians at Florida State University and Purdue University, respectively, patiently prodded and waited for this manuscript. I am honored to submit the biography to their new series at the University Press of Florida. The former director of the University Press of Florida, Meredith Morris-Babb, has never wavered support in more than two decades. Editor Sian Hunter patiently and promptly answered questions and provided good cheer and sound advice. Boyd Murphree and Robert Taylor graciously accepted a chapter on Millard Caldwell in their book on Florida governors. They provided valuable insights and suggestions. Amber Williams performed the role of proofreader and editor with grace and expertise.

As I write this, I realize that fifty-three years ago, Lynne Wheeler first appeared on my radar screen. The red-headed farmer's daughter smiled, and, with a song in her heart, I was smitten. We began dating while undergraduates at Millikin University in Decatur, Illinois. She is amazing. Friends would amend that sentence, asserting that she is also saintly, generous, and beautiful. From the Heartlands to Chapel Hill to St. Louis, from Ybor City in Tampa to Old Northeast in St. Petersburg to Valencia, Spain, and London's Bloomsbury, we have shared a wonderful life. First love, best love. Our daughters, Amy Ellen and Rebecca Lynne, have established careers and families and provide an endless source of pride and joy. Avanti!

John Belohlavek, my dear friend since 1977, read this manuscript several times and tolerated my myriad questions about the nature of biography and the craft of writing. He was the first USF faculty member I met, in the spring of 1974, when I interviewed for an assistant professorship. John arrived in 1970. He is, in the parlance of academe, a lifer. We have maintained a touching and meaningful friendship through Fulbright professorships abroad, through departmental debates, and across the decades. I dedicate this book to him. Thanks! You made a difference.

NOTES

Introduction

1. Riesman.
2. Gary Wills, "Monstre Désacré," *New York Review of Books*, 26 April 1990, 4.

Chapter 1. Child of Privilege, Bound to Duty: 1897–1943

1. Millard Fillmore Caldwell, "Application of the Florida Society of the National Society of the U.S., Sons of the American Revolution Membership," 7 November 1942. Ancestry.com.

2. Fischer, 642–44; "Family Tree & Genealogy of Millard Fillmore Caldwell," Wikitree.com.

3. Professor John Belohlavek guided me through the complicated nineteenth-century political issues. Email communication, 7 August 2019.

4. "Family Tree & Genealogy of Millard Fillmore Caldwell," Wikitree.com; Federal U.S. Censuses of 1830, 1850, 1860, Tennessee; *U.S. Sons of American Revolution Membership Applications, 1889–1970.* The author expresses his gratitude to eastern Tennessee native and longtime friend, Lester Lamon, for his help with this section.

5. J. A. Murray, "Governor's Family Retains Love of Country Life," *Tampa Morning Tribune,* 3 January 1945; Caldwell quoted in Hettie Cobb, "Millard Caldwell: Man of Legend," *Tallahassee Democrat,* 24 October 1976; *Ole Miss: 1917–1918 Yearbook.*

6. The Carson-Newman University archives contain no official record of Caldwell registered as a student, although college promotional literature claims Caldwell as an alumnus. The campus newspaper recorded that Caldwell was a commencement speaker in 1946. Email from Albert L. Lang, Special Collections

archivist, Carson-Newman University, 11 July 2016. Millard Caldwell, interview with Ray Washington; *Ole Miss*, 78, 138, 156, 166, 241.

7. "L.L.B. 1921 Millard F. Caldwell Jr." *Virginia Law Weekly*, 16 December 1948, 2; Floridasupremecourt.org, "Justice Millard Fillmore Caldwell." In the many interviews, the topic of Caldwell's military service was rarely discussed. The author would like to express thanks to Professors Connie Lester and Barbara Gannon about this topic.

8. "Populations by Counties," *The Fifth Census of the State of Florida, 1925*, 11; "Widespread Negro Exodus," *St. Petersburg Independent*, 19 April 1925; Milton described in *Florida: A Guide to the Southernmost State*, 447.

9. J. A. Murray, "Governor's Family Retains Love of Country Life," *Tampa Morning Tribune*, 3 January 1945; Hettie Cobb, "Millard Caldwell: Man of Legend," *Tallahassee Democrat*, 24 October 1976; Tindall, 111–43; Rucker, 28–46.

10. J. A. Murray, "Governor's Family Retains Love of Country Life," *Tampa Morning Tribune*, 3 January 1945; Hettie Cobb, "Millard Caldwell: Man of Legend," *Tallahassee Democrat*, 24 October 1976; email from Brian Rucker to author, 13 March 2017.

11. Caldwell quoted in Hettie Cobb, "Millard Caldwell: Man of Legend," *Tallahassee Democrat*, 24 October 1976; "Mrs. Caldwell, Wife of Former Governor, Dies at 89," *Tallahassee Democrat*, 25 February 1986; "Mrs. Caldwell Would Rather Stay on Family Plantation," *St. Petersburg Times*, 17 December 1944.

12. Caldwell quoted in Jim Hardee, "Millard Caldwell 'Tells It Like It Was,'" *Tallahassee Democrat*, 29 December 1968.

13. A. Morris, 18; Caldwell quoted in Barbara Frye, "Millard Caldwell," *St. Petersburg Times*, 27 December 1977; Jim Hardee, "Millard Caldwell 'Tells It Like It Was,'" *Tallahassee Democrat*, 29 December 1968.

14. M. Johnson, 16–17.

15. MacKay, 14.

16. A. Morris, 18.

17. Millard Caldwell, interview.

18. Ibid.; *Tallahassee Daily Democrat*, 1 May 1938; Adage quoted in Blum, 90; Letter, Congressman Caldwell to Secretary of the Navy, 16 August 1933. In the letter, Caldwell stressed "urgent need for the development of the Naval Air Station at Pensacola." Interestingly, Secretary of the Navy Claude A. Swanson ranked the Pensacola project third in importance, only after Pearl Harbor and Panama. Caldwell quoted in Franklin D. Roosevelt Library, President's Personal File, PPF, 5808.

19. Adler, 72–73, 77; "1933 Political World Series," SETH.Com; *The Political Graveyard: Index to Politicians: Caldwell*.

20. Samuel Proctor interview with Jake C. Belin, 13 August 1992, Port St. Joe, Florida. University of Florida Oral History Program.

21. Ibid.

22. Caldwell interview with Washington; Caro, 3–4, 8, 125, 196; Sikes, 70, 72, 102.

23. Gonzalez, 95.

24. "Mrs. Caldwell," *St. Petersburg Times*, 17 December 1944; Wigginton quoted in Hettie Cobb, "Millard Caldwell: Man of Legend," *Tallahassee Democrat*, 24 October 1976; Millard Caldwell interview; "Re. Millard Caldwell: Florida's 3rd District, Voting Record," Govtrack.com.

25. Tindall, 354–432; Wigginton quoted in Hettie Cobb, "Millard Caldwell: Man of Legend," *Tallahassee Democrat*, 24 October 1976; Caldwell quoted in Barbara Frye, "Millard Caldwell," *St. Petersburg Times*, 27 December 1977; Millard Caldwell interview with Ray Washington; "Millard Caldwell: Congressman," Associated Press, Florida Biographical Service, 4 December 1934, Caldwell Papers, University of Florida; Caldwell quoted in Washington interview; Caldwell quoted in Barbara Frye, "Millard F. Caldwell," *St. Petersburg Times*, 27 December 1977.

26. *Milton Gazette*, 2 January 1942; Tindall, 354–432; Hillman, 190.

27. *Florida: A Guide*, 274; "Tallahassee Funeral Custom Ended by Daily Newspaper," *St. Petersburg Times*, 20 August 1939.

28. "Florida Plantations Past: More Plantations, #9," United States Dept. of Interior, National Park Service, National Register of Historic Places Registration Form, Blackwood-Harwood Plantations Cemetery, 16 October 1999; Paisley, 5, 69, 129, 133, 135, 137, 139; Leon County GenWeb.com, "Blackwood Cemetery." The Harwood-Caldwell dairy barn now rests at the Florida Agricultural Museum at Palm Coast.

29. Caldwell quoted in Hettie Cobb, "Millard Caldwell: Man of Legend," *Tallahassee Democrat*, 24 October 1976; J. A. Murray, "Governor's Family Retains Love of Country Life," *Tampa Morning Tribune*, 3 January 1945; Jim Hardee, "Millard Caldwell 'Tells It Like It Was,'" *Tallahassee Democrat*, 29 December 1968.

30. Email from Diane Roberts to author, 6 December 2017.

31. Mrs. Caldwell quoted, "Florida's Next Governor and the First Lady Are Plantation Folks," *Tampa Morning Tribune*, 24 May 1944; Margo Tupper, "Mrs. Caldwell Would Rather Stay on Family Plantation," *St. Petersburg Times*, 17 December 1944.

32. Mormino, "World War II," 332–33.

33. Caldwell interview.

34. *Tallahassee Daily Democrat*, 9 December 1941 and 10 July 1942.

35. Mormino, "World War II," 33, 349; "Albert Bass, First Local Marine to Kill Jap," *Gadsden County Times,* 26 June 1942; Letter to the editor, Fuller Warren, *Milton Gazette,* 8 January 1942; McGovern, 216.

36. Mormino, "World War II," 333–35.

37. Ibid.

38. *Tallahassee Daily Democrat,* 21 May 1944.

Chapter 2. The Candidate and the Governor: 1943–1949

1. Washington interview with Caldwell.

2. Ibid.; Belin and Ball, 187.

3. "Caldwell Gets in Florida Governor's Race," *Tampa Morning Tribune,* 15 October 1943; *Tallahassee Daily Democrat,* 1 May 1938.

4. Ernest R. Graham papers; "Philip Graham, 48, Publisher, a Suicide," *New York Times,* 4 August 1963, 28–55.

5. "Green Qualifies in Governor's Race for 1944," *St. Petersburg Times,* 2 January 1944.

6. Washington interview with Caldwell; "Millard Caldwell," *Tallahassee Democrat,* 24 October 1976; Jim Hardee, "Millard Caldwell 'Tells It Like It Was,'" *Tallahassee Democrat,* 29 December 1968.

7. Millard Caldwell papers, P. K. Yonge Library, Box 2, expense accounts; handbill, Caldwell papers, Box 2, newspaper clippings; "Millard Caldwell to Speak in Williams Park Thursday," *St. Petersburg Times,* 16 May 1944.

8. Ibid., Caldwell papers [more info needed?], University of Florida.

9. Allen Morris, "Cracker Politics," *Panama City News-Herald,* 2 April 1944; Flynt; Colburn and Scher, 68–70.

10. Weiss, 39–77.

11. Tindall, 166–69; Mormino, "Florida's White Primary," 23–42; "Caldwell Flays White Primary Ruling," *St. Petersburg Daily Times,* 8 April 1944; "Pepper Ready to Fight Negro Vote in Primary," *Tampa Morning Tribune,* 5 April 1944; Caldwell quoted in *Pittsburgh Courier,* 1 February 1945; Clark, *Red Pepper,* 33–36.

12. "Caldwell is Close Third in the Race for Governor," *Tampa Morning Tribune,* 3 May 1944; "Governor Vote By Counties," *St. Petersburg Times,* 4 May 1944.

13. Caldwell papers, University of Florida, box 3, press releases; "Caldwell's Statement," *St. Petersburg Times,* 5 May 1944.

14. "In Electing the Governor, Vote on Facts and Not on Promises," *St. Petersburg Times,* 21 May 1944; "Millard Caldwell," *Miami Herald,* 9 May 1944.

15. "More About Caldwell," *Tampa Morning Tribune,* 24 May 1944; "Governor-elect to Confer with Local Citizens," and "Rep. Lex Green Resigns to Become Naval Officer," *St. Petersburg Times,* 21 July and 28 November 1944.

16. Radio speech, St. Petersburg, 11 October 1944, Caldwell papers, box 9, speeches 1944.

17. "Bert Ackers Makes a Wish," *Miami News,* September 10, 1948.

18. Hughes, 131–46; Touchton quoted, "Florida Senate O.K.'s Measure Favoring G.O.P.," *St. Augustine Record,* 27 May 1937; Colburn and Scher, 26–27, 59–60; Klingman, xii.

19. "Primary Registration 1942." Compiled by R. A. Gray, Secretary of State.

20. "Faithful Pinellas Republicans," editorial, *Tampa Morning Tribune,* 12 November 1944; "Clement Says GOP victory in Pinellas Would Signal County's Political Suicide," *St. Petersburg Times,* 28 October 1944.

21. Mormino, "GI Joe Meets Jim Crow," 23–42; Mormino, "World War II," 332–52; Colonel quoted, "World War II," 344.

22. Colburn and Scher, 194; Rogers, 313–15, 328.

23. "Complete Postwar Plans Prepared by Millard Caldwell," *St. Petersburg Evening Independent,* 29 August 1944; Colburn and Scher, 60.

24. Wigginton quoted in Hettie Cobb, "Millard Caldwell: Man of Legend," *Tallahassee Democrat,* 24 October 1976; Colburn and Scher, 135–36.

25. "The Vanishing Americans: Only 14 Civil War Vets Now," *St. Petersburg Times,* 6 March 1945; Gary R. Mormino, "Who Belongs on a Pedestal?" *Tampa Bay Times,* 5 July 2015.

26. *Tallahassee Daily Democrat,* 3 January 1945.

27. Ibid.

28. "Florida Welcomes New Governor with Ovation Subdued by War," *Tampa Morning Tribune,* 3 January 1945; Mormino, "World War II," 333.

29. Mormino, "GI Joe Meets Jim Crow"; "5 Negroes Found Guilty at Mabry," *Tallahassee Daily Democrat,* 4 May 1944; "Tallahassee Riot," *Pittsburgh Courier,* 14 October 1944.

30. "Text of Caldwell's Inauguration Address," *Tampa Morning Tribune,* 3 January 1945.

31. "Holland's Suit, Caldwell's Hat Cause Concern," *Tallahassee Daily Democrat,* 3 January 1945.

32. "Gov and Mrs. Millard Caldwell Give Formal Reception," "Open House at Executive Mansion," and "Two Balls Are Held in Honor of Florida's First Family," *Tallahassee Daily Democrat,* 3 January 1945.

33. Caldwell quoted in Barbara Frye, "Millard F. Caldwell," *St. Petersburg Times,* 27 December 1977.

34. Green quoted in Orrick and Crumpacker, 250; "Juanita Green, Pioneering Environmental Reporter and Activist, Dies at 93," *Miami Herald,* 3 September 2017. In Miami, she became an environmental activist and confidante to Marjory Stoneman Douglas. Davis, *An Everglades Providence,* 437, 442, 439, 574.

35. David Colburn and Richard Scher argue that while Caldwell valued loyalty, he also demanded merit, *Florida's Gubernatorial Politics*, 135. Wigginton quoted in J. A. Murray, "Governor Hard at Work for Inauguration," *Tampa Morning Tribune*, 1 January 1945; Jim Hardee, "Millard Caldwell 'Tells It Like It Was,'" *Tallahassee Democrat*, 29 December 1968. John Wigginton went on to a distinguished legal career, becoming a well-respected judge.

36. *Tampa Morning Tribune*, 27 November 1942; Kennedy, 58–60; "Strict Check to be Kept on Men Quitting Jobs to Loaf," *Key West Citizen*, 27 February 1943.

37. Colburn and Scher, 101–10, 115–24; Caldwell quoted in Jim Hardee, "Millard Caldwell 'Tells It Like It Was,'" *Tallahassee Democrat*, 29 December 1968.

38. "Hard Fighting J. Tom Watson Dies in Tampa," *Tallahassee Democrat*, 25 October 1954.

39. Shell-Weiss, 124–25; Mormino, *Hillsborough County*, 62; "Attorney General Suggests Use of Non-Union Work in Tampa Shipbuilding Plant," *St. Petersburg Times*, 13 August 1942; "5000 Workers Plan 'Walkout' to Vote," *Tampa Daily Times*, 5 November 1944; Editorial, "Soldiers and the Closed Shop," *Tampa Morning Tribune*, 26 October 1944.

40. "State of Florida On Spending Spree," *Highland News*, 27 April 1945.

41. Caldwell interview.

42. *Palm Beach Post* and *Ocala Star-Banner* quoted in "What Florida Editors Said About Caldwell Speech," *St. Petersburg Times*, 15 April 1945.

43. "New State Laws," *St. Augustine Record*, 1 July 1945; "Caldwell Says Racing Ban Blow to Florida Finances," and "Taxation Shapes Up as Big Event at State Legislature," *St. Petersburg Times*, 24 December 1944 and 1 April 1945; Malcolm B. Johnson, "Legislature is Limited in Finding New Tax Source," *St. Petersburg Times*, 25 February 1945; Caldwell quoted in "Lawmakers' Work Pleases Governor," *St. Petersburg Times*, 8 April 1945; Will M. Taer, "A Little Russia Right Here at Home," *Winter Park Herald*, 18 May 1945.

44. Allen Morris, "Caldwell Lacks Leaders in Tax Fight," *Miami News*, 29 April 1945.

45. *Tallahassee Daily Democrat*, 27 May 1945; "North and South Florida Fight Renewed," *St. Petersburg Times*, 2 June 1945.

46. Nesmith quoted in "South Florida Bloc in House Stands Pat," *Tampa Morning Tribune*, 15 June 1945; Allen Morris, "Wakulla Legislator," *St. Petersburg Times*, 16 March 1950.

47. "Why Gov. Caldwell is Wise in Calling Special Session," and "What Florida Editors Are Writing About," *St. Petersburg Times*, 2 and 10 June 1945; Williamson, 133–43.

48. "House Votes To Seat Akerman," *St. Petersburg Times*, 8 April 1947; Linda

Chapin, "Groveland Four Lawyer Deserves Belated Respect," *Orlando Sentinel*, 9 February 2016.

49. Malcolm B. Johnson, "John Proctor," *Tallahassee Daily Democrat*, 3 January 1944.

50. "Pasco Elects Pioneer Florida Legislator, 86," *Tampa Morning Tribune*, 7 June 1944; Hendley.

51. Alabama also had a single woman, Sibyl Murphree Poole, in its wartime legislature; Gary R. Mormino, "Why Mary Lou Baker Belongs in Florida Women's of Fame," *Tampa Bay Times*, 2 September 2017, "Why Mary Lou Baker Belongs in Florida Women's Hall of Fame"; "Mary L. Baker is the Only Woman Solon in State," *Jacksonville Journal*, 7 June 1944; "New Law Sponsored by Mary Lou Baker 'Frees' Married Women of State," *St. Petersburg Times*, 13 June 1943; "Mary Lou Baker Defends Use of Maiden Name," *St. Petersburg Times*, 12 February 1944; "Lets Wives Run Property," *New York Times*, 6 May 1943; "House Rejects Bill to Place Women on Jury," *Sarasota Herald-Tribune*, 22 April 1943.

52. A. Morris, 246–47; Klein, 100–101; *Tallahassee Daily Democrat*, 3 July 1942.

53. Karl, 64, 301; Allen Morris, "Legislative Chips," *Miami Herald*, 18 April 1943; quote from *Florida: A Guide to the Southernmost State*, 274; Interviews with Vernon Peeples, Tampa, 1990–2000.

54. A. Morris quote, 247, see also 72–74; Klein, 65–67, 71; Mormino and Pozzetta, 52, 61; Colburn and Scher, 72; Mormino, *Land of Sunshine*, 170.

55. Weitz, 45; *The Seventh Census of the State of Florida: 1945*, 9.

56. Klein, 56–57, 117, 142–43, 145; Catts quoted in Colburn and Scher, 127, see also 31; Sikes quoted in "Sikes, the Beloved He-Coon," *Orlando Sentinel*, 29 September 1994; "U of F: a Training Ground for Florida Politicians," *St. Petersburg Times*, 17 October 1965; Editorial, "An Example of Why Senate Reapportionment is Necessary," *St. Petersburg Times*, 2 June 1945.

57. Colburn and Scher, 172–73.

58. Gary Mormino, interview with James Clendinen, 21 April 1980. The taped interview is housed at the Special Collections, University of South Florida, Tampa.

59. Klein, 29–30, 41–45, 48–50; Orrick and Crumpacker, 348–50; Hampton Dunn, "What Dil Clarke Wants, Dil Clarke gets," *Tampa Daily Times*, 25 June 1955; Harris quoted in "Reapportionment Battle," *St. Petersburg Times*, 8 July 1945; "Johnson, Clarke, Johns are Leaders in Legislature Dictatorship," *Tampa Tribune*, 29 February 1960.

60. "Caldwell Says South Florida Faction," *Tampa Morning Tribune*, 19 July 1945.

61. Klein, 10, 117, 118–19; Weitz, 46–47; *Tampa Morning Tribune*, July 1, 1945; Watson quoted in *Fort Pierce News-Tribune*, 1 July 1945; legislator quoted in

Hampton Dunn, "What Dil Clarke Wants," *Tampa Daily Times*, 25 June 1955; Brackin quoted in *St. Petersburg Times*, 25 July 1945.

62. Klein quoted 112; "Senators Scuffle in Restaurant," and "North Florida Blasts Bolters," *Tallahassee Daily Democrat*, 19 and 24 July 1945; Senator Riddle quoted in "Senate Squabble," *Fort Lauderdale Daily News*, 26 June 1945; *St. Augustine Record*, 24 July 1945.

63. Johnson, "I Declare," *Tallahassee Democrat*, 28 May 1965; *Ocala Star-Banner*, 3 July 1945; Allen Morris, "How Legislators Straddle Debatable Bills," *Miami News*, 5 May 1945; Pooser quoted in "Rep. Pooser," *St. Petersburg Times*, 24 May 1945.

64. "Broward Fills Dime Barrels," and "Broward Representatives 'Unaware' of Dime Barrel," in *St. Petersburg Times*, 3 and 17 July 1945.

65. "Move to Create 49th State Dies in Caucus," *St. Petersburg Times*, 11 July 1945; Editorial, *Belle Glade Herald*, reprinted in *Miami Herald*, 11 June 1945; Governor Arnold quoted in *Miami Herald*, 11 June 1945; Martin Anderson, "Keep Your State Capital," *Orlando Sentinel*, quoted in the *Winter Haven Daily Chief*, 13 July 1945; "Orlando Tells Tallahassee It doesn't want the Capital," *Tampa Morning Tribune*, 12 July 1945; "The Governor Straddles," editorial, *Tampa Morning Tribune*, 11 July 1945; "At Long Last—Broward Gets Senator," *Fort Lauderdale Daily News*, 25 July 1945.

66. "Reapportionment Battle and Political Hopes," *St. Petersburg Times*, 8 July 1945; "Longest Session Ends," *Tallahassee Democrat*, 25 July 1945; Caldwell quoted in Colburn and Scher, 173; "South Florida Wins," *Tampa Morning Tribune*, 25 July 1945.

67. Davis quoted in *Lakeland Ledger*, 24 July 1945; "Partial Reapportionment," *Tampa Morning Tribune*, 26 July 1945; Allen Morris, "Legislators bitter," *Panama City News-Herald*, 29 July 1945; Caldwell quoted in Tom Wagy interview, 18 June 1956. The author thanks Martin Dyckman for the transcription of his interview.

68. Editorial, *St. Petersburg Times*, 9 June 1945.

69. Caldwell telegram, V-J Proclamation, 10 August 1945, Florida Memory Project; Caldwell telegram to President Truman, 13 August 1945, Florida Memory Project; Mormino, "Peace at Last," 40–41.

70. *Okaloosa News-Journal*, 5 May 1944; Sikes, 192.

71. Mormino, "World War II," 348–49.

72. R. Johnson, 1–10, 18.

73. Kevin Starr pioneered the study of dream states in his magisterial series of books. See *Americans and the California Dream; The Dream Endures: California Enters the 1940s; Embattled Dreams: California in War and Peace, 1940–1950*.

74. Ibid., *The Dream Endures* and *Embattled Dreams*.

75. "Peace is Crisis, Warns Caldwell," *Miami Herald*, 16 August 1945; Editorial, "What Has Happened?" *St. Petersburg Times*, 21 September 1948.

76. "Peace is Crisis, Warns Caldwell," *Miami Herald*, 16 August 1945.

77. Editorial and "Fate in 1946," *Miami Herald*, 22 November 1944 and 1 January 1946; Claude Pepper diary, 24 January 1946.

78. "Caldwell Asks Vets to Help Fight Domestic Enemies," and "Gov. Caldwell Forsees End of Boom Prosperity," *Miami Herald*, 4 April 1946.

79. "Florida Faces Best Period in History," *Tampa Morning Tribune*, 16 January 1946.

80. "Senate Race Tops Official Vote Recount," *Tampa Morning Tribune*, 16 May 1946; "Spessard Holland Named US Senator," *Tallahassee Daily Democrat*, 25 September 1946; "Spessard L. Holland Dies," *New York Times*, 7 November 1971.

81. Colburn and Scher, 42–43.

82. Shofner, 21–22, 52.

83. Ibid., 171–72.

84. J. A. Murray, "Canaveral Port Site Now Is Remote Fishing Village," *Tampa Morning Tribune*, 17 February 1946.

85. Mormino, *Land of Sunshine*, 156–58; Rabac, 28–29.

86. John Matson, "Why Does NASA Launch Space Shuttles from Such a Weather-Beaten Place?" *Scientific American*, 15 July 2009.

87. Ibid.; "Missile at Cocoa," *Miami Herald*, 25 July 1950.

88. Bilstein and Taylor, 47–49; Dietrich, 87.

89. *Bradenton Herald*, 21 August 1945; "Hurricane Bombing Base Offered," *Miami Herald*, 9 August 1945; Claude Pepper diary, 9 August 1945.

90. Arsenault, 597–628.

91. Ibid., 623–24; "Local Stores Announce Plans for Miami's Postwar Future," *Miami Herald*, 15 August 1945; Mormino, *Land of Sunshine*, 238.

92. Mormino, *Land of Sunshine*, 229–53; *St. Augustine Record*, 16 July 1945; Patterson, *Mosquito Wars*, 73–76.

93. Mormino, "GI Joe Meets Jim Crow," 40; Weitz, 57–69.

94. Clark, "Civil Rights Leader Harry T. Moore," 167–70; Harry T. Moore, "Development and Activities of NAACP in Florida during 1945," *Florida Sentinel*, 12 January 1946; "Teachers Win Raise," *The Crisis* 50 (November 1942): 360; Price, 53.

95. Correspondence quoted in Green, 5; Green quoted in Michael Browning, "Moore Didn't Receive Recognition," *Palm Beach Post*, 16 August 1999.

96. "Lynching to be Lost Crime by 1940," *Tampa Morning Tribune*, 12 January 1930; Hobbs, 157.

97. The best treatment of the Payne tragedy and its consequences is Jack E. Davis, "'Whitewash,'" 277–98.

98. Letter, Harry T. Moore to Governor Caldwell, 17 October 1945. Caldwell papers, Lynching File, 1945, Series 576, Box 48.

99. Green, 57, 68; Weitz, 61; Hobbs, 172.

100. Davis, "'Whitewash,'" 283.

101. Waldrep, 173.

102. Ibid.; Davis, "'Whitewash,'"; Caldwell quoted in "Collier's editors defend editorial," *St. Petersburg Times*, 29 June 1949; *Colliers* quoted in "Colliers's editors deny any malice in Caldwell editorial," *Tampa Morning Tribune*, 30 June 1949; "Jury gives Caldwell $100,000," *Tampa Morning Tribune*, 1 July 1949; Caldwell quoted in "Gov. Lashes at Criticism from Tampa," *Tampa Morning Tribune*, 13 February 1946; "Caldwell given $50,000 in libel suit settlement," *St. Petersburg Times*, 25 August 1949.

103. "Caldwell Refuses to Oust Sheriff," and "Caldwell Disdains Timid, Honeyed Talk; Once Jolted Tampa," *Tampa Morning Tribune*, 25 October 1947 and 24 April 1958.

104. Davis quoted in "Lynching in Florida?" *Gainesville Sun*, 3 September 2005; "Jury Scores Sullivan, Asks Caldwell to Enforce Law," *Miami Herald*, 8 February 1946; Caldwell quoted in "Caldwell Tells Miami He's No Policeman of Gambling," *Tampa Morning Tribune*, 5 December 1945.

105. Davis, "'Whitewash,'" 289; Green, 55, 60–61; Hobbs, 170.

106. "Caldwell Stands Behind his Tax Program," *Tampa Morning Tribune*, 3 January 1946.

107. Lamb, 12–17; Rampersad, 99–109.

108. *New York Times* quoted in Lamb, 61–100; "Negro Stars *Join* Royals in Florida," *Tampa Morning Tribune*, 5 March 1946.

109. "Governor Hits Losing Teams," *Tampa Daily Times*, 16 November 1945; Governor Still Wants 'Real' Football Team at Florida," *Tampa Morning Tribune*, 6 April 1946.

110. "Miami," *Tampa Morning Tribune*, 6 November 1946.

111. Ibid.; "Gaither Named Rattler Coach," *St. Petersburg Times*, 9 March 1946.

112. "FSU's Start Was Truly Significant," *Pensacola News Journal*, 17 January 2014; Caldwell quoted in Jim Joanos, "Garnet & Old," www.nolefan.org/garnet.

113. "Caldwell Hits Surrender of State's Rights," *Tampa Morning Tribune*, 5 July 1946.

114. "Governor Stays on Sidelines in Equal Rights Discussion," *Miami Herald*, 18 April 1946.

115. Millard Caldwell, "Florida still undeveloped," *State Government* reprinted

in *Florida Times-Union*, 4 March 1945; "Caldwell Disdains Timid, Honeyed talk," *Tampa Morning Tribune*, 24 April 1958; "Deficit of $9,700,000 forecast," *Tampa Morning Tribune*, 1 May 1947; Caldwell interview.

116. Orrick and Crumpacker, 246–49, 288; *Tampa Morning Tribune*, 26 June, 16 July, 24 August 1947.

117. McCullough quoted in "'Gopher' Meat Bolsters Diet at County Negro Boys' Home," *Tampa Morning Tribune*, 8 May 1947. Headlines gathered from *Tribune* files, 1946–47.

118. Colburn, 238; *Education and the Future of Florida*, 168.

119. "Caldwell Calls for Extra Millions as Legislature Opens," *Tampa Morning Tribune*, 9 April 1947; Caldwell quoted in "Governor Says teachers will be Worse Off," *St. Petersburg Times*, 18 May 1947; Allen Morris, "Governor's Message Fails to Yield Ammunition for His Foes," *Orlando Morning Sentinel*, 3 April 1947.

120. Dyckman, *Floridian*, 43–44.

121. Ibid.; Wagy, 31–32; "Credit for Approval of School Bill Given to Caldwell and FEA," *Tampa Morning Tribune*, 4 May 1947; M. Johnson, 18.

122. Mormino, "History of Methods of Election and Disenfranchising Devices," article prepared for the American Civil Liberties Union in the United States District Court for the Middle District of Florida, Fort Myers Divisions; *Brenda Johnson, et al., Plaintiffs v. De Soto County Board of Commissioners*, (1995); 1–60; 1907 Florida Laws, ch. 6874, 4573, section 2; 1947 Florida Laws, ch. 32726, 7; Letter, 21 April 1945, Ben D. Griffin, Executive Secretary of the Florida State Teachers Assoc. to Governor Millard Caldwell, Millard Caldwell papers, Citizens Committee, Education; Dyckman, *Floridian*, 44; Colburn, 26; Letter, C. A. Barnett to Governor Caldwell, 28 January 1948, Millard Caldwell papers, Box 11.

123. "Gainesville Jammed with Students, Vets, and Babies," *Tampa Morning Tribune*, 11 September 1946.

124. "1600 Excess at Florida U: No Room for Them at FSCW," *Tampa Morning Tribune*, 17 August 1946; "GI Bill Played Huge Part in FSU," *Tallahassee Democrat*, 16 October 2007; "Gainesville Jammed with Students, Vets, and Babies," *Tampa Morning Tribune*, 11 October 1946; Kreher, 34.

125. William Oliver interview with Millard Caldwell, 8 July 1975, Tallahassee. Central College closed its doors in 1947, reopening as Central Baptist College in 1952.

126. Ibid.; Sellers, 253, 273.

66; "Girls' College," *Tampa Morning Tribune*, 28 April 1947; J. Earle Bowden, "FSU's Start was Truly Historic," *Pensacola News Journal*, 17 January 2014.

127. "Co-education Question Sent Back to Board of Control," *Gainesville Daily*

Sun, 30 August 1944; Dyckman, *Floridian,* 44; Colburn and Scher, 249; "GI Bill," *Tampa Tribune,*13 June 1994.

128. Patterson, "Hurston Goes to War," 166–83; Letter, Zora Neale Hurston to Walter White, 24 November 1942, NAACP Papers, pt. 9, ser. B, Discrimination in the U.S. Armed Forces, 1918–1955, Roll 12, 106.

129. "School Lunch Pact Signed with Florida," *Florida-Times Union,* 4 July 1946.

130. "Medical Education," [more info needed] 79.

131. "Southern States to Study Joint Use of Negro College" and "Caldwell Tells Senators No Race Issue," in *Tampa Morning Tribune,* 13 January 1948 and 13 March 1948; "The One Best Way," *Time,* 16 February 1948: 75; Egerton, 430–31; "Southern States Act on Negro Students," *Tallahassee News-Democrat,* 1 February 1948. Florida authorized $40,000 during the 1947–48 school year, which allowed over 200 black students to attend classes assigned at other state schools but not offered at Florida A&M College. Caldwell quoted in "Caldwell States South's Case," *Tampa Morning Tribune,* 8 April 1948; Oral history interview with John Ivey, 21 July 1990, Southern Oral History Program, University of North Carolina.

132. "Governor Asks Millions in New Taxes," *Gainesville Daily News,* 18 May 1947; "Greatest Appropriations Act Clears Legislature," *Tallahassee Daily Democrat,* 23 May 1947; "Deficit of $12,000,000 is Estimated for State," *Miami Herald,* 3 June 1947; "Caldwell Asks Tax Raise of 34 million," and "Caldwell Lays State Deficit to Public's Tax Indifference," *Tampa Morning Tribune,* 3 and 12 June 1947; "Florida Sales Tax Plan Dies," *Palm Beach Post Times,* 7 May 1947.

133. Hoover, 68.

134. "Odham Describes Bribe Offer," *Miami Herald,* 22 July 1947.

135. Hoover, 68–78; "Papy Trial," and "Papy Acquitted of Bribery Charges," *Miami Herald,* 20 and 25 July 1947.

136. "Jury Scores Sullivan," *Miami Herald,* 8 February 1946; "Caldwell Tells Miami He's No Policeman of Gambling," *Tampa Morning Tribune,* 5 December 1945; "Wild and Wooly Days of Boom Gaming," *Miami Herald,* 17 February 1946.

137. Mormino and Pozzetta, 4, 281–84, 302, 215; "Gambling Interests Rated No. 1 Power in Tampa Politics," *Tampa Morning Tribune,* 5 October 1947.

138. Caldwell quoted in *Pittsburgh Courier,* 10 February 1945; "Florida Should Be Among First to Let Negroes Vote in Primaries," *St. Petersburg Times,* 23 February 1945.

139. Mormino, "Florida's White Primary"; Dyckman, *Floridian,* 45.

140. Farris, 270–74; Papers of the NAACP, Voting Rights Campaign, part 4, reel 6, 789–800; Matthews and Prothro, 148; Harry T. Moore, "Development and

Activities of NAACP during 1945," *Florida Sentinel*, 12 January 1946; Caldwell quoted in "Caldwell Answers," *St. Petersburg Times*, 7 November 1946.

141. Grunwald, 197–236; "Park Created Despite Watson," *St. Petersburg Times*, 15 June 1947; Davis, *Everglades Providence*, 380–99; "Watson to Take Glades Park Fight to U.S. Supreme Court," *Tampa Morning Tribune*, 17 December 1947.

142. Davis, *Everglades Providence*, 389; Grunwald, 212; "Cattlemen Ask Federal Flood Funds," *Tampa Morning Tribune*, 8 October 1947; "Cattlemen Deep in Water," *Sarasota Herald-Tribune*, 7 October 1948; Davis, *Everglades Providence*, 387.

143. *Tampa Morning Tribune*, 12 December 1947.

Chapter 3. The Wild Ride: Florida at the Crossroads, 1948

1. "Former Florida Grid Coach Named Chief of Army in Greece," "Dodocanese Maintain Loyalty to Greece," and "Masaryktown Hall is Symbol of Czechoslovakian Spirit," *Tampa Morning Tribune*, 7 February 1948, 23 December 1947, and 13 March 1948; "Tampa Italians Urge Friends to Oust Reds," *Tampa Daily Times*, 1 April 1948; "Cuban Politicians," *Tampa Morning Tribune*, 2 May 1948.

2. David McCullough, "Give 'em Hell," *New York Times*, 25 September 2010.

3. Minister quoted in Leuchtenburg, "Conversion of Harry Truman," 60; "Florida Democrats are Polled on Truman Stand," *Tampa Morning Tribune*, 7 March 1948; Ex-supporter letter quoted in Weitz, 57.

4. McCullough, 639–40, 645; Egerton, 475; Pleasants, 453; Weitz, 56.

5. Caldwell, "The South and Civil Rights," Caldwell papers, University of Florida, Box 10.

6. 19 March 1948 letter, Governor J. Strom Thurmond to Governor Millard F. Caldwell, Caldwell Papers, carton 15.

7. Cohodas, 131; *Tallahassee Daily Democrat*, 7 February 1948; Pleasants, 443; *New York Times*, 7 February 1948.

8. Truman quoted in White and Maze, 260–70; Claude Pepper diary, January 1945, Claude Pepper Library, Florida State University.

9. "The South and Wallace," *Tampa Morning Tribune*, 9 September 1948; "Wallace Will Test South's Hospitality," *Miami Herald*, 28 August 1948; "Wallace Pelted with Eggs," *New York Times*, 31 August 1948.

10. Toney, 6–29; "2500 Hear Wallace Rap Both Parties," and "Crowd Shouts Viva Wallace," *Tampa Morning Tribune*, 14 and 18 February 1948; "Robeson Sings and Talks Here," *Tampa Daily Times*, 5 October 1948; "Wallace Party Seen as Hope of 'Common Man,'" *St. Petersburg Times*, 27 June 1948; White and Maze, 270–82; Gen. Lowry Urges Tampans to Boycott Wallace Speech," and "Police Blacklist of Wallace's Friends Charged," *Tampa Morning Tribune*, 17 and 5 February 1948.

11. Max Howard, Letter to editor, "God Bless America," *Tampa Morning Tribune*, 8 February 1948; "Wallace Hit in Repudiation of AFL," *Miami Herald*, 3 February 1948.

12. "General Lowry Urges Tampans to Boycott Wallace Speech," and "Tribune Talkies," *Tampa Morning Tribune*, 17 and 21 February 1948; "General Calls for Boycott," *Lakeland Ledger*, 17 February 1948; Toney, 65.

13. "Sumter deLeon Lowry: The Perfect Guardsman," *Department of Military Affairs: The Home of the Florida National Guard*, 12 June 2012; Lowry, *Ole* 93; "General Lowry Calls For More Patriotism," *Tampa Morning Tribune*, 12 November 1950; "Lowry Urges State Schools To Fight Reds," *Tampa Daily Times*, 13 December 1950.

14. "Gov. Caldwell Opposed Bolt," *St. Petersburg Times*, 6 June 1948; Pleasants, 439–40, 445–46.

15. "Split Delegates Leave on Separate Trains," *St. Petersburg Times*, 4 July 1948.

16. "Pepper Says He Won't Quit Demos to Support Wallace," *Tampa Morning Democrat*, 30 December 1947; "General Willing to Take 'Honest Draft,'" and "Senator Pepper Enlists in Move for Eisenhower," *St. Petersburg Times*, 4 July 1948; "Ike's No Puts Pepper in Even Worse Spot," *St. Petersburg Times*, 10 July 1948; W. H. Lawrence, "Oratory is Torrid," *New York Times*, 13 July 1948; Pleasants, 450; Clark, *Red Pepper*, 22–36, 80–95.

17. "Why We are Against Pepper for President," "Pepper Bandwagon Stalled," and "Pepper Gets a Going Over," *St. Petersburg Times*, 12, 13, and 16 July 1948; "Frank D. Upchurch Sr. Dies at 92," *St. Augustine Record*, 2 June 1986; Pleasants, 461.

18. "Watson Wants To Be Governor," *Miami Herald*, 11 April 1948; "Hard Fighting J. Tom Watson Dies," *Tallahassee Democrat*, 25 October 1954; "Watson Urges Dixiecrats to Organize, *St. Petersburg Times*, 20 July 1948; Colburn and Scher, 124–25; Dyckman, *Floridian*, 77.

19. "Thurmond Blasts 'Party Loyalty' at Wildwood," *Lakeland Ledger*, 6 September 1948.

20. Sheppard quoted in "Democratic Row Flares in Open on Civil Rights," *St. Petersburg Times*, 16 July 1948; Frederickson, 109–10, 140, 145; Egerton, 479; Pepper quoted in *St. Petersburg Times*, 15 July 1948; *New York Times*, 15 July 1948; Cohodas, 164.

21. Pepper quoted in "Floridians, with No Place to Go, Give Russell 19 votes," *St. Petersburg Times* and "Democratic Row Flares in Open on Civil Rights," *St. Petersburg Times*, 15 and 11 July 1948; Pleasants, 454.

22. White and Maze, 204, 225, 256; "Republican Wants Wallace Under Arrest," *Tampa Morning Tribune*, 12 June 1947.

23. "Caldwell Asks for Freedom in Teaching," *St. Petersburg Times*, 5 September 1948; "Caldwell on Communists," editorial, *Tampa Morning Tribune*, 25 September 1948; Henrietta and Nelson Poynter, "Democratic Party," *St. Petersburg Times*, 15 July 1948; Editorial, "Caldwell," *Lakeland Ledger*, 10 September 1948.

24. Schmidt, 149; Frederickson, 157; Clark, *Red Pepper*, 81; Pleasants, 459; "Upchurch Raps Truman," *St. Petersburg Times*, 12 August 1948; "Watson Urges Dixiecrats to Organize," *St. Petersburg Times*, 20 July 1948; Bartley, 92–93; "Frank D. Upchurch Sr.," *St. Augustine Record*, 4 June 1986; "Wallace Must Form Party to Get on Florida Ballot," *Tampa Morning Tribune*, 41 December 1947; "The Special Session," *Lakeland Ledger*, editorial, 12 September 1948.

25. Schmidt, 149; "Gov. Caldwell Issues Call to Legislature," "Legislative Battle Seen on Wallace," and Caldwell quoted in "Senate Votes to Put Wallace on Florida's Ballot," *Tampa Morning Tribune*, 11, 12, and 15 September 1948; "Voters in Florida May Get Clear Cut Choice in Vote for President this Fall," and "Legislators Will Find Wallace at Their Elbows," *St. Petersburg Times*, 13 and 19 September 1948; Pleasants, 459–60; "Special Session," *Lakeland Ledger*, 19 September 1948.

26. Pleasants, 459–62; "Caldwell, Pepper Will Support Ticket," *St. Petersburg Times*, 16 July 1948.

27. Pleasants, 467; Orrick and Crumpacker, 260; "Truman for President," *St. Petersburg Times*, 15 July 1948.

28. "Klan Parades but Fails to Scare Negroes," "Cross Burning at Fort Myers Rally," and "Cross Burning in Pinellas," *Tampa Morning Tribune*, 2 November, 14 February, and 1 June 1948; "Caldwell Orders Probe of Klan's Covered Licenses," *St. Petersburg Times*, 3 November 1948.

29. Orrick and Crumpacker, 260; "Upchurch Predicts Thurmond Will Beat Truman," *Daytona Beach Morning Journal*, 15 October 1948; Danese, 200–201.

30. Pleasants, 468–69; "Pinellas Goes for Dewey," *St. Petersburg Times*, 3 November 1948; "Political Miracle Fails Truman," *St. Petersburg Evening Independent*, 1 November 1948; Weitz, 69–70.

31. Florida Department of State, Division of Elections, Official Vote—State of Florida General Elections—1948 Tabulated by Counties (Tallahassee, 1948).

32. *Tampa Morning Tribune*, 6 June, 15, 16, 22, 28 July, 3 November 1948; "Mayoria a Favor de H. Wallace en Ybor City y West Tampa," *La Gaceta*, 3 November 1948; Schmidt, 87; "Tampa was infamous for its Corrupt Elections," *Tampa Bay Times*, 11 November 2018.

33. "Caldwell and Watson Bury Axe," *Tampa Morning Tribune*, 10 November 1948.

34. "Demos' Caucus Okays Akerman for Legislature," *Orlando Morning Sentinel*, 8 April 1947; Pepper quoted in *Florida Times-Union*, 15 April 1947.

35. King, 79.

36. "An Inconvenient Truth: Central Florida's Role in Civil-Rights Movement," *Orlando Sentinel*, 14 January 2018; Colette Bancroft, "Lasting Impact of Gilbert King's 'Devil in the Grove,' Almost Didn't Happen," *TBT*, 17 January 2019.

37. Colburn, 21–25; Arsenault and Mormino, 161–92; Mormino, *Land of Sunshine*, 1–10; Pleasants, 470; Leuchtenburg, *White House*, 210–11.

38. "Miami to have All-Negro Court," *Tampa Daily Times*, 20 April 1950; "City Will Add Four Negroes to Police Force," *St. Petersburg Times*, 13 June 1947; "Miami Shows the Way in Improved Race Relations," and "Florida's First Negro Catholic Priest," *Florida Sentinel*, 16 December 1950 and 24 February 1949; Mormino, "World War II," 345; Bush, 107–46.

39. Pleasants, 470–71; "Southern Democrats Urged to Back GOP" and "GOP Shows Strength," *St. Petersburg Times*, 14 October and 7 November 1946; "GOP Pinellas Totals Worry County Demos," *Tampa Morning Tribune*, 7 November 1946; "Better Government," *St. Petersburg Independent*, 5 November 1948.

40. *Fort Myers News-Press*, 18 October 1944. See Brown. Collier County Democrats remained loyal—even in briefly—to the Democratic Party, supporting Truman in 1948. "Collier County Joins In Truman Landslide," *Collier County News*, 5 November 1948.

41. Colburn, 58–63; Pleasants, 472–73; Frederickson, 206; See Kallina biography of Kirk.

42. "Election's Over, Caldwell Answers Fuller Warren," *St. Petersburg Times*, 6 June 1948.

43. A. Morris, 205; Morris, "Governor Warren Inherits Problems, Finds Little Money Left in the Till," *Tallahassee Democrat*, 8 January 1949; Caldwell quoted in "Caldwell Says He'll Stay Out of Governor's Race," *Tampa Morning Tribune*, 9 October 1947; M. Johnson, 17; *Miami Herald*, 30 May 1948.

44. "Caldwell says he'll go back to farm after Jan. 4," *Tampa Morning Tribune*, 3 December 1948; Letter from M. A. Whitaker to Governor Caldwell, 29 May 1946, Caldwell papers.

45. Letters, W. J. Sears to Hon. Millard Caldwell, and Gov. Caldwell to W. J. Sears Jr., 6 and 8 February 1945; Letter, Gov. Caldwell to Dr. W. A. Bagwell, 5 June 1945, Millard Caldwell Papers, University of Florida.

46. "Done Up Classy in Tallahassee," *Time*, 17 January 1949, 17; Clements, 266.

47. "Done Up Classy in Tallahassee," *Time*, 17 January 1949, 17.

48. *The Statistical History*, 12–13.

49. Lessing, 66; Mormino, *Land of Sunshine*, 127–30.

50. Arsenault and Mormino, "From Dixie to Dreamland," Table 9.9, p. 170.

51. Arsenault and Mormino, 165, 175, see Table 9.4; Census of Population: 1950, II, part 10, Florida, 29; Dietrich, 22–25.

52. Dietrich, 151.

Chapter 4. Citizen, Cold Warrior, Civil Defense Director, and Judge: 1950–1970

1. *Miami Daily News,* 6 June 1949; Caldwell quoted in "Don't Count Millard Caldwell Out as Foe for Senator Pepper," *Tampa Morning Tribune,* 24 April 1949; Clark, *Red Pepper,* 106, 108.

2. "Caldwell Counts Self Out of Race for Governor"; "Millard Caldwell Bows Out of Governor's Race," "Caldwell Would Delay State Medical, Dentistry Schools," *Tampa Morning Tribune,* 22 September 1951, 3 September 1959, and 22 November 1950; "Caldwell On Farm," "Caldwell May Be In 1960 Race," *Tampa Tribune,* 5 January 1949 and 1 March 1959.

3. "Truman Appoints Caldwell Head of U.S. Civilian Defense," *Tampa Morning Tribune,* 2 December 1950; McEnaney, 11–39.

4. Dahlgren, 1–12; "Teachers Angered with Oaths," *Orlando Sentinel,* 4 March 1948; Chapter 25046 *Florida Statute: Acts of 1948.*

5. Caldwell quoted in "Memo to Times Writers," *St. Petersburg Times,* 3 June 1951.

6. Rose, 24, 211.

7. Ibid.; Letter, L. Wilkinson, Acting Chairman, to Millard Caldwell, Administrator, January 19, 1951, Herman H. Lehman Papers, New York Public Library; "Caldwell Asks $3,150,000 Florida Civil Defense Funds," *Tampa Morning Tribune,* 5 January 1951; Matthew Dallek, "Fear Rears its Head in Race for Nomination," *Politico,* 29 April 2008; "Florida Called On for Funds to Construct Air Raid Shelters," *St. Petersburg Times,* 5 January 1951; "Civil Defense: Bomb Shelters Away," *Time,* 3 September 1951, 22; Blazich, 113–14.

8. McEnaney, 141–46; Oral interview with Martin L. Friedman, December 5, 1963, Harry S. Truman Library; Wilson, 210; Letter, George Scott, La Grange chapter NAACP to Johnson, U.S. Senate papers, Nominations series, Lyndon B. Johnson Library, University of Texas, Austin, Texas. Email from archivist Liz Talbot, 18 January 2018.

9. McEnaney, 141–46; Wilson, 210.

10. Raymond Mason, "A Powerful Man Craved Little but Gave a Lot," *Florida Times-Union,* 21 February 1999; Jahoda, 132–33; "What the Branches Are Doing," *Crisis* 58 (March 1951), 194.

11. Jacob C. Belin worked alongside Ball for several decades. Sam Proctor interview with Jacob C. Belin.

12. "Ed Ball's 1920s Ideas Booed," *Florida Times-Union,* 25 June 1981.

13. Mason; "Death Claims Ed Ball," *Tallahassee Democrat,* 25 June 1981; Roberts quoted in "Ed Ball's 1920s Ideas Booed," *Florida Times-Union,* 25 June 1981; "Ed Ball's 1920s Ideas Booed," *Florida Times-Union,* 25 June 1981; Belin and Ball, 8, 32–37.

14. Burnett, 107.

15. "Ed Ball at 91, Embattled, Implacable," *New York Times,* 11 March 1979; Belin interview; Dyckman, *Floridian,* 98; Belin and Ball, 9, 62–64, 197.

16. Dyckman, *Floridian,* 98; Roberts, 231; Collins quoted in "Ed Ball's Empire Endures," *Orlando Sentinel,* 22 June 1986.

17. Martin Dyckman, "Tax Reform Fight is Nothing New," *St. Petersburg Times,* 16 December 2001.

18. Belin interview; Dyckman, *Floridian,* 31–32; Danese, 80–82.

19. Belin interview; Roberts, 232; Dyckman, *Floridian,* 47–48; MacKay, 15.

20. "Ed Ball at 91"; "Vengeful Ball," *Florida Times-Union,* 25 June 1981; Claude Pepper diary, 22 January 1946.

21. Pepper quoted in *Tampa Morning Tribune,* 5 April 1944; Clark, *Red Pepper,* 11–21; Danese, 137–43; Claude Pepper diary, 4 April 1944; Letter, 31 January 1938, Fuller Warren to Claude Pepper, Fuller Warren Papers, University of Florida, Correspondence with Claude Pepper.

22. Clark, *Red Pepper,* 22–36.

23. Danese, 137–55; Claude Pepper diary, 22 March 1944; Clark, *Red Pepper,* 370–83.

24. Claude Pepper diary, 2, 5, 11, and 12 January 1946; Crispell, 38–39.

25. Claude Pepper diary, 27 May 1946; Crispell, 42.

26. Letters, James A. Ball Jr. to Millard Caldwell, August 1, 1949, and Millard Caldwell to Ball, August 3, 1949, E. J. Bodman to Millard Caldwell, July 25, 1949, Millard Caldwell Papers, University of Florida.

27. Clark, *Red Pepper,* 106.

28. Ibid., 120–55; Crispell, 4–12; Smathers quoted in Ritchie interview; Truman quoted in Danese, 20.

29. Crispell, 57–58; *Tampa Morning Tribune,* 28 March and 1 April 1950; *Tampa Daily Times,* 9 March 1950.

30. "Anything Goes," *Time,* April 1950, 27–28. J. Earle Bowden, the longtime editor and publisher of the *Pensacola News-Journal,* covered the 1950 race as a young reporter. He told this author in the late 1980s about how the origins of the infamous Smathers remarks; Crispell, 66.

31. "General Lowry Calls for More Patriotism," *Tampa Morning Tribune,* 12 November 1950; "Lowry Urges State Schools To Fight Reds," *Tampa Daily Times,* 13

December 1950; "Smathers Wants Reds Under Surveillance," *Tampa Daily Times*, 29 July 1950; Danese, 137.

32. Claude Pepper diary, 7 January 1944; Belin interview.

33. Smathers interview; "The Red Record of Claude Pepper," Special Collections, University of South Florida Library.

34. Danese, 146–47, 204.

35. Ibid., 149.

36. Covington, 40; Buffalo Tiger quoted in "Miccosukee Indians Threaten Open War," *SN*, 6 February 1959; Dina Gilio-Whitaker, "When Mad Bear Met Fidel," Indiancountrytoday.com, 14 July 2015.

37. "Caldwell Says He's Not Seeking Governor's Post," *Tampa Tribune*, 14 November 1958.

38. Editorial, "Caldwell Backs Stevenson," *Lakeland Ledger*, 24 May 1956; "Caldwell says Stevenson Democrat's strongest choice," *St. Petersburg Times*, 26 April 1956; Kefauver quoted in "Dark Horses," *Chicago Tribune*, 29 May 1956.

39. Fontenay, 257–58; "Estes Concedes He 'lost head' in Florida Test," *St. Petersburg Times*, 18 June 1956; Kefauver quoted in "Estes Links Ike With Adlai," *Chicago Tribune*, 26 May 1956.

40. Wagy, 140–41; Dyckman, *Floridian*, 51–52.

41. "Caldwell Cites Nation's Role in Free World," *Orlando Sentinel*, 13 January 1953; "Caldwell Says He's Against Industrialization of Florida," *Tampa Tribune*, 8 December 1956; Editorial, "No Buggy Ride, Thanks," *Tampa Tribune*, 21 May 1960; "Governors Says Southern Way of Life Endangered," *St. Petersburg Times*, 14 August 1945; "Old Home Too Far Gone," *Tallahassee Democrat*, 3 August 1958.

42. Caldwell quoted in Hettie Cobb, "Millard Caldwell: Man of Legend," *Tallahassee Democrat*, 24 October 1976; "Caldwell May be in 1960 Race," *Tampa Tribune*, 1 March 1960.

43. Wagy, 132–43; Dyckman, *Floridian*, 190–97; "Millard Caldwell Bows Out of Governor's Race," *Tampa Tribune*, 3 September 1959; Caldwell quoted in "Caldwell Says He's Not Interested in Seeking Governor's Post," *Tampa Tribune*, 14 November 1958.

44. "The Caldwell Decision," editorial, *Tampa Tribune*, 4 September 1959.

45. Dyckman, *Floridian*, 198.

46. "Segregation No Issue," *St. Petersburg Times*, 24 January 1960; Dyckman, *Floridian*, 198–206; "Bryant Hits Court on States' Rights," *Tampa Morning Tribune*, 22 August 1957; "That Florida's Growth May Continue," editorial, *St. Petersburg Times*, 22 May 1960; "Collins Cites Interposition Stand in 1957," *St. Petersburg Times*, 21 May 1960; "Carlton and Bryant Clash in Views on Racial Issues in TV broadcast," *St. Petersburg Times*, 22 May 1960. Ironically, observed

the *St. Petersburg Times* on 3 January 1954, Bryant's "three daughters did attend racially integrated schools and Bryant didn't even raise an eyebrow, much less his voice."

47. Dyckman, *Floridian*, 198–200; Caldwell quoted in *Tampa Tribune*, 16 January 1959.

48. Carlton quoted in "Gov. Collins' Support Welcomed by Carlton," *St. Petersburg Times*, 21 May 1960; "C. Farris Bryant," *New York Times*, 6 March 2002; Caldwell and Collins quoted in "Caldwell Says Bryant Best Qualified to Fight Integration," *Tampa Tribune*, 20 May 1960.

49. "Capping a Distinguished Career" and "Caldwell Rises to Bench," *St. Petersburg Times*, 15 and 2 February 1962; "Caldwell Named to Florida Bench," *Virginia Law Weekly*, 1 March 1962.

50. "Ex-Governor Caldwell Named to Supreme Court by Bryant," *Tampa Tribune*, 14 February 1962; "After Hobson Steps Down," *St. Petersburg Times*, 18 February 1962.

51. "Justice Caldwell Assails U.S. High Court," *Tampa Times*, 22 October 1962; "Caldwell Blasts Civil Rights Law," and "Justice Caldwell Says U.S. Suffers from 'Moderation,'" *Tampa Tribune*, 24 October 1964 and 28 February 1965; Allen Morris, "Millard Caldwell Takes Charge," *Lakeland Ledger*, 25 February 1962; "Retiring Justice," *Florida Times-Union*, 5 January 1969; Caldwell quoted in "Cicero's Prognosis," an address to the annual meeting of the Association of American Physicians, 9 October 1965. If one googles "Caldwell and Cicero's Prognosis," scholars and lay persons question the validity of Caldwell's classical quotations.

52. Brown and Manley, 262.

53. "Millard Caldwell a Superb Citizen," *Pensacola News-Journal*, 17 November 1968; Graves, 61.

54. Caldwell letter quoted in Thomas [not in refs], 227.

55. Caldwell, "Cicero's Prognosis," October 1954, Caldwell Papers, University of Florida.

56. Speeches, 1964, Box 10, Millard Caldwell Papers, University of Florida.

57. Brown and Manley, 267.

58. Dyckman, *Most Disorderly*, 18–19, 25; Belin and Ball, 154–56, 180–83.

59. "FSU to Move Eppes Statue, Wants to Strike Roberts," *Tallahassee Democrat*, 17 July 2018.

60. Ibid.; Brown and Manley, 254, 261–62; Newbeck, 120, 194; Caldwell quoted in "Millard F. Caldwell," *New York Times*, 25 October 1984; Adkins, 45–46.

61. Marshall, 8, 37; "Former FSU President Stanley Marshall Dies at 91," *Tallahassee Democrat*, 9 June 2014.

62. Phillips.

63. Kallina, 189.

64. Ibid.; Gary R. Mormino, "The Ghosts of Race and Bomb Shelters in Florida," *Tampa Bay Times*, 23 August 2017.

65. "Carswell 'Shocked' That Confirmation Being Jeopardized," *Sarasota Herald-Tribune*, 16 March 1970; "Carswell Says He Was 'Incorporator' of Club," *St. Petersburg Times*, 28 January 1970; Rabby, 75–76, 252–53; Dyckman, *Floridian*, 254–55.

66. "Carswell Called Foe of Women's Rights," *New York Times*, 30 January 1970; Marshall, 124–25.

67. "Carswell to Run for U.S. Senate," *Panama City News-Herald*, 21 April 1970; "Hawthorn, 402–26; "Carswell Arrested by Vice Squad," *New York Times*, 27 June 1976; Kallina, 186–91.

68. Kallina, 1–46.

69. Ibid., 27–29, 48; Caldwell interview.

70. Kallina, 164–65; Noll, 356–82.

71. Nixon and Cramer quoted in Kallina, 165; Noll and Tegeder, 258–67; Caldwell quoted in Burnett, 200.

Chapter 5. Conclusion: Who Belongs on the Pedestal?

1. Adkins, 72; Talbot "Sandy" D'Alemberte, "Introduction: Constitution Revision Symposium," *Florida State University Law Review* 5 (Fall 1977): 1.

2. Caldwell quoted in Barbara Frye, "Millard F. Caldwell," *St. Petersburg Times*, 27 December 1977; "Public Employee Union Bargaining Attacked," *Tampa Tribune*, 8 July 1977.

3. "Former governor dies at 87," *Tampa Tribune*, 24 October 1984; "Millard F. Caldwell," *New York Times*, 25 October 1984; "Mary Caldwell, Wife of Former Governor, Dies at Age 89," *St. Petersburg Times*, 25 February 1986; Morris and O'Connell quoted in "Former Gov. Millard Caldwell Dies," *Tallahassee Democrat*, 24 October 1984; Johnson quoted in Hettie Cobb, "Millard Caldwell: Man of Legend," *Tallahassee Democrat*, 24 October 1976.

4. "Mobile Home," *Tallahassee Democrat*, 15 July 1986.

5. E. Morris, 4.

6. Letter to editor, Richard Damashek, "Not 'Complicated'—He's a Racist," *Tampa Bay Times*, 1 September 2017.

7. "Artists and Scholars Debate the Rush to Topple Statues," *New York Times*, 19 August 2017; "In S. Fla., Racial Epithets in Tense Protests Over Confederate Street Names," *Politico*, 22 June 2017.

8. "Is Broward Named for a Racist?" and "'Racist' Statue of Broward County's

Namesake to be Removed," *Sun-Sentinel,* 29 September and 10 October 2017; Proctor.

9. Mormino, "Hero," 7.

10. Ibid., 7–9, "Statue of Dr. Gorrie," *Tampa Morning Tribune,* 12 April 1914.

11. Gary R. Mormino, "Who Belongs on the Pedestal?" *Tampa Bay Times,* 3 July 2015; Tingley, 476–508.

12. Dyckman, *Floridian,* 190–197; Wagy, 12; E. Morris, 4.

13. "Civil Rights Leader Mary McLeod Bethune to Replace Confederate General," *Tampa Bay Times,* 22 February 2018; "Committee to Ponder Fate of Incoming Confederate Statue," "Hundreds Protest Confederate Statue," and "Lake Honors Newspaperwoman," *Orlando Sentinel,* 28 June and 1 November 2018 and 10 August 2019.

14. Belohlavek, 116; "Tubman Beats Jackson on the $20 Bill," *Wall Street Journal,* 6 September 2017.

15. "George Washington, Dashing Young Colonel," *Washington Post,* 14 December 2018; "Robert E. Lee's Namesake," Inside Highered.com, 23 August 2017.

16. "Debate over Renaming Russell Building," *Atlanta Journal-Constitution,* 27 August 2018; "Revisiting the Unpleasant History of the Man Behind the Russell Building's Name," *Washington Post,* 29 August 2018; "Why is Walter F. George Disappearing from Mercer's Law School?" 13WMAZ, 22 October 2018; "Filibuster Against Anti-Lynching Bill," loc.gov/resource/hec.23959, Library of Congress.

17. "Race and Party Politics, Senator Fulbright and Justice Black," Historyhalf. com, 7 March 2011; Brian Palmer, "What Does an Exalted Cyclops Do?" Slate. com, 30 June 2010.

18. Allman, 358; Hobbs, 35; "Anti-Lynching Bill," Associated Press, *Tampa Morning Tribune,* 25 January 1938.

19. "Pepper Grows More Liberal as Time Passes," Documenting the American South, Jack Bass interview with Claude Pepper; "Why It Took a Century to Pass an Anti-Lynching Law," *Washington Post,* 28 December 2018.

20. Paul Galloway, "Pointing Out Some Other Peccadillos," *Chicago Tribune,* 7 March 1989.

21. "The Groveland Four: A 'Shameful Chapter' Continues," editorial, *Orlando Sentinel,* 13 December 2018; "Gov. Rick Scott Still Hasn't Pardoned Florida's 'Groveland Four,'" and "'Miscarriage of Justice': Florida Finally Pardons Four Black Men Accused of Rape in 1949," *Washington Post,* 5 December 2018 and 11 January 2019.

22. "B. K. Roberts' Granddaughters 'Disheartened' by FSU Panel Recommendations," *Tallahassee Democrat,* 18 May 2018; "Eppes Family Responds," WCTV. TV, 18 July 2018.

23. Roberts, 55; email from Diane Roberts to author, 6 December 2017.

24. Roberts, 55–56; Wilson quoted in Chang and Hart, 65; Gerald Easley, "Springtime Tallahassee Evolving with More Diversity," *Tallahassee Democrat*, 23 March 2015; Mormino, "Hero," 7–8.

25. The author appreciates the efforts of Michelle Hearn, a senior curator at the Museum of Florida History, in tracking down the Florida Master Site File for the Caldwell building. "Shrewd Banker Fred McCord Dies at 92," *Tallahassee Democrat*, 1 December 2014.

26. "State Government," *Florida Times-Union*, 5 March 1945; "Former State Governor Millard Caldwell Dies," *Boca Raton News*, 24 October 1984; "Memo to Times Writers," *St. Petersburg Times*, 4 June 1951; Ron Cunningham, "Understanding that a Great State Requires Great Universities," *Gainesville Sun*, 10 February 2013.

27. Editorial, "Amazing Career: Millard Caldwell," *Pensacola News-Journal*, 17 November 1968.

BIBLIOGRAPHY

Archives and Collections

Claude Pepper Papers, Florida State University Libraries, Tallahassee, Florida.

Franklin D. Roosevelt Presidential Library, Archives. Hyde Park, New York.

Fuller Warren Papers, P. K. Yonge Library. University of Florida. Gainesville, Florida.

Herbert H. Lehman Papers, New York Public Library.

Lyndon B. Johnson Presidential Library, University of Texas, Austin, Texas.

Millard Fillmore Caldwell, Administration Files, Florida State Archives, Tallahassee, Florida.

Millard Fillmore Caldwell Papers, University of Florida. Smathers Libraries, Gainesville, Florida.

NAACP Papers, Pt. 4, Voting Rights Campaign.

NAACP Papers, Pt. 9, Discrimination in the U.S. Armed Forces, 1918–1955.

Public Documents

The Fifth Census of the State of Florida Taken in the Year 1925. Tallahassee: T. J. Appleyard, 1926.

"Primary Registration of 1942," R. A. Gray, Secretary of State.

The Seventh Census of the State of Florida, 1945. Tallahassee: N. Mayo, Commissioner of Agriculture, 1946.

Interviews

Belin, Jake. Interview with Sam Proctor, 13 August 1992, Port St. Joe, Florida, Samuel Proctor Oral History Program, University of Florida.

Caldwell, Millard Fillmore. Interview with Ray Washington, 23 November 1981, Tallahassee, Samuel Proctor Oral History Program, University of Florida.

Caldwell, Millard Fillmore. Interview with William Oliver, Tallahassee, 8 July 1975.

Friedman, Martin. Interview with Charles T. Morrissey, Washington, D.C., 5 December 1963, Harry S. Truman Library.

Ivey, John. Interview with John Egerton, Nashville,21 July 1990, Southern Oral History Program Collection, University of North Carolina.

Smathers, George A. Interview with Donald A. Ritchie, 1 August 1989, Senate Historical Office, Washington, D.C.

Secondary Sources

Adkins, Mary E. *Making Modern Florida: How the Spirit of Reform Shaped a New Constitution.* Gainesville: University Press of Florida, 2016.

Adler, Melissa. *Cruising the Library: Perversities in the Organization of Knowledge.* New York: Fordham University Press, 2017.

Allman, T. D. *Finding Florida: The True History of the Sunshine State.* New York: Atlantic Monthly Press, 2013.

Arsenault, Raymond. "The End of the Long Hot Summer: The Air Conditioner and Southern Culture." *Journal of Southern History* 50 (November 1984): 597–628.

Arsenault, Raymond O., and Gary R. Mormino. "From Dixie to Dreamland: Demographic and Cultural Change in Florida, 1880–1980." In *Shades of the Sunbelt: Essays on Ethnicity, Race, and the Urban South,* edited by Randall M. Miller and George E. Pozzetta, 161–92. Westport: Greenwood Press, 1988.

Bartley, Numan V. *The New South, 1945–1980.* Baton Rouge: Louisiana State University Press, 1996.

Belin, J. C., and Braden Lee Ball. *The Edward Ball We Knew: An Untold Story of the Man Who Really Discovered Florida.* Pensacola: University of West Florida Foundation Pioneer Series, 1998.

Belohlavek, John M. *Andrew Jackson: Principle and Prejudice.* New York: Routledge Press, 2016.

Bilstein, Roger E., and Mary Amelia Taylor. "Aerospace." In *New Encyclopedia of Southern Culture,* Vol. 22 *Science and Medicine,* edited by Charles Reagan Wilson, 47–49. Chapel Hill: University of North Carolina Press, 2012.

Blazich, Frank Arthur, Jr. "Economics of Emergencies: North Carolina, Civil Defense, and the Cold War, 1940–1963." Ph.D. dissertation, The Ohio State University, 1963.

Blum, John Morton. *V Was for Victory: American Culture during World War II*. New York: Harcourt Brace Jovanovich, 1976.

Brown, Canter, Jr., and Walter W. Manley. *Supreme Courts of Florida, 1917–1972*. Gainesville: University Press of Florida, 2006.

Brown, Loren G. *Totch: A Life in the Everglades*. Gainesville: University Press of Florida, 1993.

Burnett, Gene M. *Florida's Past: People & Events that Shaped the State*. Sarasota: Pineapple Press, 1986.

Bush, Gregory W. *White Sand Black Beach: Civil Rights, Public Space, and Miami's Virginia Key*. Gainesville: University Press of Florida, 2016.

Caro, Robert. *Means of Ascent: The Years of Lyndon Johnson*. New York: Alfred A. Knopf, 1990.

Chang, Perry, and Joyce Hart. *Florida: (Celebrate the States)*. New York: Cavendish Square Publishing, 2007.

Clark, James C. "Civil Rights Leader Harry T. Moore and the Ku Klux Klan in Florida." *Florida Historical Quarterly* LXXIII (October 1994): 167–82.

———. *Red Pepper and Gorgeous George: Claude Pepper's Epic Defeat in the 1950 Democratic Primary*. Gainesville: University Press of Florida, 2011.

Clements, Patricia Lasch. *Legacy of Leadership: Florida Governors and Their Inaugural Speeches*. Tallahassee: Sentry Press, 2005.

Cohodas, Nadine. *Strom Thurmond and the Politics of Southern Change*. Macon: Mercer University Press, 1995.

Colburn, David R. *From Yellow Dog Democrats to Red State Republicans: Florida and Its Politics since 1940*. Gainesville: University Press of Florida, 2007.

Colburn, David R., and Richard K. Scher. *Florida's Gubernatorial Politics in the Twentieth Century*. Tallahassee: University Presses of Florida, 1980.

Covington, James W. "The State of Florida, The Florida Indians: 1954–1961." *Tequesta* 46 (1986): 35–47.

Crispell, Brian Lewis. *Testing the Limits: George Armistead Smathers and Cold War America*. Athens: University of Georgia Press, 1999.

Dahlgren, Robert L. "Red Scare in the Sunshine State: Anti-Communism and Academic Freedom in Florida Public Schools, 1945–1960." *Cogent Education* 3 (2016): 1–12.

Danese, Tracy E. *Claude Pepper and Ed Ball: Politics, Purpose, and Power*. Gainesville: University Press of Florida, 2000.

Dáte, S. V. *Quiet Passion: A Biography of Senator Bob Graham*. New York: Tarcher/Penguin, 2004.

Davis, Frederick Rowe. *Banned: A History of Pesticides and the Science of Toxicology*. New Haven: Yale University Press, 2014.

Davis, Jack E. *An Everglades Providence: Marjory Stoneman Douglas and the American Environmental Century.* Athens: University of Georgia Press, 2009.

———. "'Whitewash' in Florida: The Lynching of Jesse Payne and its Aftermath." *Florida Historical Quarterly* LXVIII (January 1990): 277–98.

Dietrich, T. Stanton. *The Urbanization of Florida's Population: An Historical Perspective of County Growth, 1830–1970.* Gainesville: Bureau of Economic and Business Research, 1978.

Dyckman, Martin A. *Floridian of His Century: The Courage of Governor LeRoy Collins.* Gainesville: University Press of Florida, 2006.

———. *A Most Disorderly Court: Scandal and Reform in the Florida Judiciary.* Gainesville: University Press of Florida, 2008.

Education and the Future of Florida. Tallahassee: 1947.

Egerton, John. *Speak Now Against the Day: The Generation Before the Civil Rights Movement.* New York: Alfred A. Knopf, 1994.

Farris, Charles. "The Re-Enfranchisement of Negroes in Florida." *Journal of Negro History* 39 (October 1954): 259–83.

Fischer, David Hackett. *Albion's Seed: Four British Folkways in America.* New York: Oxford University Press, 1989.

Florida: A Guide to the Southernmost State. New York: Oxford University Press.

Flynt, Wayne. *Cracker Messiah: Governor Sidney J. Catts of Florida.* Baton Rouge: Louisiana University Press.

Fontenay, Charles L. *Estes Kefauver: A Biography.* Knoxville: University of Tennessee Press, 1980.

Frederickson, Kari. *The Dixiecrat Revolt and the End of the Solid South, 1932–1968.* Chapel Hill: University of North Carolina Press, 2001.

Gonzalez, Darryl J. *The Children Who Ran for Congress: A History of Congressional Pages.* Denver: Praeger, 2010.

Graves, Karen. *And They Were Wonderful Teachers: Florida's Purge of Gay and Lesbian Teachers.* Urbana: University of Illinois Press, 2009.

Green, Ben. *Before His Time: The Untold Story of Harry T. Moore, America's First Civil Rights Martyr.* New York: Free Press, 1999.

Grunwald, Michael. *The Swamp: The Everglades, Florida, and the Politics of Paradise.* New York: Simon & Schuster, 2006.

Hawthorn, Billy. "Cramer v. Kirk: The Florida Republican Schism of 1970." *Florida Historical Quarterly* 68 (April 1990): 402–26.

Hendley, J. A. *History of Pasco County.* Dade City: n.p. 1927.

Hillman, John. *The International Tin Cartel.* London: Routledge, 2010.

Hobbs, Tameka Bradley. *Democracy Abroad, Lynching at Home: Racial Violence in Florida.* Gainesville: University Press of Florida, 2015.

Hoover, Michael. "'$500 and a Case of Scotch': The 1947 Florida Legislative Bribery Scandal." *Selected Proceedings of the Florida Conference of Historians* 12 (2005): 68–78.

Hughes, Edward M. "Florida Preachers and the Election of 1928." *Florida Historical Quarterly* 67 (October 1988): 131–146.

Jahoda, Gloria. *Florida.* Nashville: American Assoc. for State and Local History, 1976.

Johnson, Malcolm B. *I Declare! A Collection of Editorial Commentaries.* Tallahassee: Tallahassee Democrat, 1983.

Johnson, Rody. *The Rise and Fall of Dodgertown: 60 Years of Baseball in Vero Beach.* Gainesville: University Press of Florida, 2008.

Kallina, Edmund F., Jr. *Claude Kirk and the Politics of Confrontation.* Gainesville: University Press of Florida, 1993.

Karl, Frederick B. *The 57 Club: My Four Decades in Florida Politics.* Gainesville: University Press of Florida, 2010.

Kennedy, Stetson. *Southern Exposure.* New York: Doubleday, 1946.

King, Gilbert. *Devil in the Grove.* New York: Harper Perennial, 2013.

Klein, Kevin N. "Guarding the Baggage: Florida's Pork Chop Gang and its Defense of the Old South." Ph.D. dissertation, Florida State University, 1995.

Klingman, Peter. *Neither Dies Nor Surrenders: A History of the Republican Party of Florida, 1867–1970.* Gainesville: University Presses of Florida, 1984.

Kreher, R. A. *We Are the Boys of Old Florida: A Pictorial History of the University of Florida.* Self-published, 1980.

Lamb, Chris. *The Untold Story of Jackie Robinson's First Spring Training.* Lincoln: University of Nebraska Press, 2004.

Lessing, Lawrence. "State of Florida." *Fortune,* February 1948, 65–72, 211–13.

Leuchtenburg, William. "The Conversion of Harry Truman." *American Heritage* 42 (November 1991): 59–62.

———. *The White House Looks South: Franklin D. Roosevelt, Harry S. Truman, and Lyndon B. Johnson.* Baton Rouge: Louisiana State University Press, 2005.

Lowry, Sumter L. *Ole 93.* Tampa: s.n. 1970.

MacKay, Buddy, and Rick Edmonds. *How Florida Happened: The Political Education of Buddy Mackay.* Gainesville: University Press of Florida, 2010.

Marshall, J. Stanley. *The Tumultuous Sixties: Campus Unrest and Student Life at a Southern University.* Tallahassee: Sentry Press, 2006.

Mason, Raymond K. *Confusion to the Enemy.* Gainesville: University of Florida Press, 1976.

Matson, John. "Why Does NASA Launch Space Shuttles from Such a Weather-Beaten Place?" *Scientific American:* 15 July 2009.

Matthews, Donald R., and James Warren Prothro. *Negroes and the New Southern Politics.* New York: Harcourt, Brace & World, 1966.

McCullough, David. *Truman.* New York: Touchstone Book, 1993.

McEnaney, Laura. *Civil Defense Begins at Home: Militarization Meets Everyday Life in the Fifties.* Princeton: Princeton University Press, 2000.

McGovern, James. *The Emergence of a City in the Modern South: Pensacola, 1900–1945.* DeLeon Springs: E. O. Painter, 1976.

Mormino, Gary R. "GI Joe Meets Jim Crow: Violence and Reform in World War II Florida." *Florida Historical Quarterly* 73 (July 1994): 23–42.

————. "Hero Today." *FORUM: The Magazine of the Florida Humanities Council* 28 (Fall 2004): 6–9.

————. *Hillsborough County Goes to War.* Tampa: Tampa Bay History Center, 2001.

————. "A History of Florida's White Primary." In *Sunbelt Revolutions: The Historical Progression of the Civil Rights Struggle in the Gulf South, 1866–2000,* edited by Samuel C. Hyde Jr. 133–152. Gainesville: University Press of Florida, 2003.

————. *Land of Sunshine, State of Dreams: A Social History of Modern Florida.* Gainesville: University Press of Florida, 2005.

————. "Peace at Last." *FORUM: The Magazine of the Florida Humanities Council* XXI (Fall 1999): 40–41.

————. "World War II." In *The History of Florida,* edited by Michael Gannon, 332–52. Gainesville: University Press of Florida, 2013.

Mormino, Gary R., and George E. Pozzetta. *The Immigrant World of Ybor City: Italians and Their Latin Neighbors in Tampa, 1885–1985.* Urbana: University of Illinois Press, 1987.

Morris, Allen. *Reconsiderations: Second Glances at Legislative Events.* Tallahassee: Office of the Clerk, House of Representatives, 1987.

Morris, Edmund. *Dutch: A Memoir of Ronald Reagan.* New York: Random House, 1999.

Newbeck, Phyl. *Virginia Hasn't Always Been for Lovers: Interracial Bans and the Case of Richard and Mildred Loving.* Carbondale: Southern Illinois University Press, 2005.

Noll, Jody Baxter. "'We Are Not Hired Help': The 1968 Statewide Teacher Strike and the Formation of Modern Florida." *Florida Historical Quarterly* 95 (Winter 2017): 356–82.

Noll, Steven, and David Tegeder. *Ditch of Dreams: The Cross Florida Barge Canal and the Struggle for Florida's Future.* Gainesville: University Press of Florida, 2009.

Ole Miss: 1917–18 Yearbook. Oxford, Miss.: 1918.

Orrick, Bentley, and Harry C. Crumpacker. *The Tampa Tribune: A Century of Journalism*. Tampa: University of Tampa Press, 1998.

Paisley, Clifton. *From Cotton to Quail: An Agricultural Chronicle of Leon County, Florida, 1860–1967*. Tallahassee: University Presses of Florida, 1968.

Patterson, Gordon. "Hurston Goes to War: The Army Signal Corps in Saint Augustine." *Florida Historical Quarterly* 74 (Fall 1995): 166–83.

———. *The Mosquito Wars: A History of Mosquito Control in Florida*. Gainesville: University Press of Florida, 2004.

Phillips, Kevin. *The Emerging Republican Majority*. New York: Arlington House, 1970.

Pleasants, Julian. "Claude Pepper, Strom Thurmond, and the 1948 Presidential Election in Florida." *Florida Historical Quarterly* 76 (Spring 1998): 439–473.

Price, H. D. *The Negro and Southern Politics: A Chapter of Florida History*. New York: New York University Press, 1957.

Proctor, Samuel. *Napoleon Bonaparte Broward: Florida's Fighting Democrat*. Gainesville: University of Florida Press, 1950.

Rabac, Glenn. *City of Cocoa Beach: The First Sixty Years*. Wiona, Minn.: Apollo Books, 1986.

Rabby, Glenda Alice. *The Pain and the Promise: The Struggle for Civil Rights in Tallahassee, Florida*. Athens: University of Georgia Press, 1999.

Rampersad, Arnold. *Jackie Robinson: A Biography*. New York: Alfred Knopf, 1997.

Riesman, David. *The Lonely Crowd: A Study of the Changing American Character*. New Haven: Yale University Press, 1950.

Roberts, Diane. *Dream State: Eight Generations of Swamp Lawyers, Conquistadors, Confederate Daughters, Banana Republicans, and Other Florida Wildlife*. Gainesville: University Press of Florida, 2004.

Rogers, William W. "The Great Depression." In *The History of Florida*, edited by Michael Gannon, 313–32. Gainesville: University Press of Florida, 2013.

Rose, Kenneth. *One Nation Underground: The Fallout Shelter in American Culture*. New York: New York University Press, 2001.

Rucker, Brian. *Treasures of the Panhandle: A Journey through West Florida*. Gainesville: University Press of Florida, 2011.

Schmidt, Henry M. *Henry A. Wallace: A Quixotic Crusade*. Syracuse: Syracuse University Press, 1960.

Sellers, Robin. *Femina Perfecta: The Genesis of Florida State University*. Tallahassee: Florida State University Foundation, 1995.

Shell-Weiss, Melanie. *Coming to Miami: A Social History*. Gainesville: University Press of Florida, 2009.

Shofner, Jerrell H. *History of Brevard County*. I. Stuart: Brevard Historical Commission, 1995.

Sikes, Bob. *He-Coon: The Bob Sikes Story*. Pensacola: Perdido Bay Press, 1984.

Starr, Kevin. *Americans and the California Dream*. New York: Oxford University Press, 1973.

———. *The Dream Endures: California Enters the 1940s*. New York: Oxford University Press, 1997.

———. *Embattled Dreams: California in War and Peace*. New York: Oxford University Press, 2002.

Stern, Maxine, editor. *FSU Voices: An Informal History*. Tallahassee: Florida State University, 2002.

The Statistical Atlas of the United States: From Colonial Times to the Present. New York: Basic Books, 1976.

Tindall, George Brown. *The Emergence of the New South, 1913–1945*. Baton Rouge: Louisiana State University Press, 1967.

Tingley, Charles. "Another Invisible Man: Alexander H. Darnes, M.D." *Florida Historical Quarterly* 94 (Winter 2016): 476–508.

Toney, Jared G. "Tampa Latins and 1948." Master's thesis, University of South Florida, 2006.

Wagy, Thomas R. *Governor LeRoy Collins of Florida: Spokesman of the New South*. Tuscaloosa: University of Alabama Press, 1985.

Waldrep, Christopher. *The Many Faces of Judge Lynch: Extralegal Violence and Punishment in America*. New York: Palgrave Macmillan, 2002.

Weiss, Nancy. *Farewell to the Party of Lincoln*. Princeton: Princeton University Press, 1983.

Weitz, Seth A. "Bourbon, Pork Chops, and Red Peppers: Political Immorality in Florida, 1945–1968." Ph.D. dissertation, Florida State University, 2007.

White, Graham, and John Maze. *Henry A. Wallace: His Search for a New World Order*. Chapel Hill: University of North Carolina Press, 1995.

Williamson, Edward. *Florida Politics in the Gilded Age, 1877–1893*. Gainesville: University Presses of Florida, 1976.

Wilson, Sondra Kathryn, ed. *In Search of Democracy: The NAACP Writings of James Weldon Johnson, Walter White, and Roy Wilkins (1920–1977)*. New York: Oxford University Press, 1999.

INDEX

Page numbers in *italics* refer to illustrations.

GARY R. MORMINO taught history at the University of South Florida (Tampa and St. Petersburg) for more than four decades. He is the author of *Land of Sunshine, State of Dreams: A Social History of Modern Florida* and coauthor, with George Pozzetta, of *The Immigrant World of Ybor City: Italians and Their Latin Neighbors in Tampa, 1885–1985*. He is a scholar-in-residence at the Florida Humanities Council. In 2015, he was awarded a Lifetime Achievement in Writing.

Florida in Focus

EDITED BY ANDREW K. FRANK

Books in this series provide original and lively introductions to a range of topics in Florida history. Written by established scholars and using original research, the books draw upon current scholarly developments to situate subjects in a broad historical context.

Before the Pioneers: Indians, Settlers, Slaves, and the Founding of Miami, by Andrew K. Frank (2017)

Millard Fillmore Caldwell: Governing on the Wrong Side of History, by Gary R. Mormino (2020)